WWII + VI

A kid's memories of war and postwar

Johan Zwaan

ISBN: 978-1-64314-538-9 (Paperback)
        978-1-64314-539-6 (E-book)

AuthorsPress
California, USA
www.authorspress.com

FOREWORD

Fulfilling a promise to my children and grandchildren, who often
have questions about my life as a kid during World War II, I started
to write this book on June 6, 2019, the 75th Anniversary of D-Day,
the greatest invasion the world has ever seen. Seven thousand ships,
150,000 troops, 4,000 American and British deaths on the very first day.

The courage of the men, who jumped from the landing ships
into the sea, sometimes drowning with their heavy equipment,
and stormed the beaches under heavy fire from artillery,
machine guns and rifles, is unimaginable. I could not stop
thinking about it with a sense of awe and thankfulness.

It astounded me to learn how little the current generation, including
my kids, knows regarding the war. It asked sacrifices of the soldiers,
whose life was interrupted and whose families suffered. It changed
the course of the United States and her position in the world forever.

I thank my daughter Vicky for her help with the photos and
my sons, Alex (all the good ones are his) for the drawings
and Andrew for assisting me with work on the computer.

I dedicate this book to my fellow travelers on this adventure, my
siblings, Kees (deceased), Jan, Pim and Irene (deceased).

Contents

ABBREVIATIONS

AMA: American Medical Association: Countrywide voluntary organization of physicians.

BBC: British Broadcasting Corporation: The BBC had many divisions broadcasting in non-English languages. For instance, Radio Oranje (Radio Orange) transmitted in Dutch, not just the news, but also coded messages for the Resistance.

B.S.: The Binnenlandse Strijdkrachten. (Dutch Internal Forces): After the capitulation of the German forces, the Resistance basically became Dutch police forces.

Gestapo: Geheime Staatspolizei (Secret National Police). This organization was created in 1933 by combining all the local security police agencies into one national police. Eventually it became under the administration of the SS.

Holland: The name commonly used for our country. However, the formal name is The Netherlands.

NSDAP: Nationalsozialistische Deutsche Arbeiterpartei (National Socialist German Labor Party). The German Fascist Party, Hitler's Party.

NSB: Nationaal Socialistische Beweging (National Socialist Movement): The fascist political party started in Holland in 1931, similar in ideas to the German NSDAP, but independent from it. In 1936 the party gained almost 8% of the votes, but a year later this percentage had been halved. When Holland had been occupied by the Germans in 1940, many of the NSB members did collaborate.

W.A.: Weer Afdeling (Security Division): Uniformed volunteer NSB members for protection of members at meetings, etc.

SS: Schutzstaffel (Protection Squadron): The SS started as a small group of volunteers from the NSDAP providing security at party meetings, Saal-Schutz. It grew to a formidable organization of terror, security, and security in Germany and later in occupied countries. There were several major divisions. The Waffen SS (Armed SS), which operated as Army units. The Allgemeine SS (general SS) acted as general police and particularly enforced the racial laws. The Totenkopfverbande–or SS-TV was in charge of the concentration camps. Smaller units were the SD (Sicherheits Dienst or Security Service) and the Gestapo. The strength of the organization of some 200 members in 1925 had grown to 800,000 towards the end of the war.

SHAEF: Supreme Headquarters Allied Expeditionary Forces. The highest command structure during the war in Europe.

CHAPTER ONE

First Days

IT WAS THE sound that woke me up—a continuous droning that did not let up. Then I heard the radio, softly, and my parents talking. I hopped out of bed, walked through the bedroom, and looked out of the window. It was barely getting light, long before the sun was getting up, and it promised to be a nice day. The sky was still bluish-gray, and there were no clouds. Dawn is a long-drawn-out affair in Holland because the country is much higher up on the globe than you think, about at the same altitude as Nova Scotia. The noise became clearer and louder, and when I looked up, I saw hundreds of airplanes flying over, obviously the source of the noise. Later I learned that they were carrying paratroopers to occupy airfields and bridges toward the west of the country so that the attack of the German army would not be slowed down. I ran downstairs and saw my parents sitting at the dining room table, looking very serious. My mother was crying with tears running down her cheeks, a very unusual thing for her. She heard me come in, and she turned around. She said, "Oh my god, Hannetje, we are at war." My dad told me that the Germans had just invaded Holland. It was Friday, May 10, 1940. I was five years old. It was the first day of my life that I remember from dawn to dusk in great detail.

We (my parents and their four sons) had moved into a new home on Het Eind, maybe a year or so earlier, coming from a home on the Havendijk, at the other side of the old part of the city of Gorinchem (more commonly named Gorkum for short). The houses on our new street were very mixed, as were the people living there. It was far from a uniform suburb. The first house was a greengrocer's store and home. The greengrocer's name was Brouwershaven. Later his daughter Dit took over. She knew and still knows everything about old Gorkum. Then followed a family home in which the head of the household being a cantankerous guy was the boss of a small workplace where they made not only sails for boats but also tents and tarps.

Then came the office of a newspaper and a store of textiles. On the second floor of this store lived a cranky widow, Mrs. Wittmer. Her balcony looked out over our garden and our home with my dad's medical practice. Our other neighbor was Hotel Modern. At the far end of the street close to the gate going to the river, there was a bakery, a photographer, a large store selling ship supplies, the Salvation Army headquarters, and so on.

The first house, where I was born, was only vague in my memories, in little bits and pieces. There was a dumbwaiter in the corner of the dining room on the second floor going down to the kitchen. I know it because I tried to crawl in it and got stuck. In the alley behind the house, there was a butcher of chickens, rabbits, and the like; and I recall sitting on my haunches next to his shed, watching what he was doing. He would grab a rabbit by the hind legs and hit it in the neck with a heavy stick to kill it. Then he'd cut its throat and skin and clean it, all the while explaining to me what he was doing and what the various organs were. Maybe that was where I got my later interest in anatomy. I remember being stung in my rear end by a bee on the small balcony behind the house. And then there was Geertje, the maid who stayed with us for many years until she got married and who later would faithfully come to visit, never forgetting my mother's birthday. There was the other maid with long hair loaded with lice, not so unusual in those days. They dropped in droves on the edge of the bathroom sink, to my fascination and my mother's horror. I do remember a car trip we made on a Saturday to visit my grandparents in Zeist. My dad stopped the car opposite their home and told me to stay put, but I was so impatient that I jumped out anyway and smacked into a bicyclist. Of course, we both fell. Dad hit me once but firmly on my behind, and that was the only time he ever did.

Our new house on Het Eind was much bigger than the old house, with plenty of room for our family with four brothers, all born in a four-year period from 1934 to 1938. There were two front doors, one led via a few steps down to a semibasement, where my dad's office was located. You walked through a vaulted area with very thick walls, extra fortified by a large and never used built-in safe as part of its front wall. To the right was the patient waiting area with windows whose lower ledges were just at street level. Climbing on the bench against the front wall and looking through one of the two low windows, our eyes were right next to the feet of people passing by. To the left was the practice of my dad, who was a family physician. Next to the practice's entrance was a stone staircase going up to a portal with the house door much more ornate than the office door. On each side of the door was a glass-in-lead window. Our living area was at this level. All bedrooms were at the third level, and a very large attic followed. The floors were connected by a series of stairs; the tallest was between the living and bedroom floors. There were no elevators. Pim, our youngest brother, improvised one almost immediately: he would drop down on his belly, tighten his abdominal muscles, and slide down the stairs like a sled on a ski slope.

Het Eind was called that way because it is located at the end of a narrow shopping street, De Langendijk. On one side were tall very old row houses, ours being one of them. The other side of the street had a long line of linden trees, and behind those, stairs went down to the water of the harbor. The water was dirty and probably a culture of many microorganisms. As in most old cities, rats were plentiful. The bottom steps were always wet and slippery from the green algae growing there. More than once, one of us drowned or fell into the harbor. Most of the time, we were fished out of the water by the ice-cream vendor who often stood with his cart at the end of Het Eind, trying to sell his wares. It was a miracle that none of us picked up some disease from the contaminated water. This is where the small Linge River—running right through the center of the old city and ending at a lock's two large sluice doors—joins the very wide Merwede River, one of the end branches of the Rhine.

The day became more exciting. Groups of Dutch soldiers started to come through, and one platoon on motorcycles with sidecars took a smoking break right in our portal. They set up machine guns on tripods at the edge of the harbor and settled down on our stone steps. My mom cooked a large pot of *nasi goreng* (like fried rice but with more eggs and meat in it) to feed them all. The lunch was interrupted by the weekly arrival of a traveling peddler who sold needles, matches, shoelaces, and other little necessities of life out of a large wooden box that he carried around. Obviously, you could get the same things cheaper in stores, particularly the Franse Bazaar (French Bazaar), only half a block away. And I am sure that buying from the peddler was a bit of charity from my mother's part. The peddler had with him his young adult daughter who was mentally retarded. To get to the house door, they had to step around and over the legs of the soldiers sitting on the stairs of the portal. The daughter was shy and got very scared, so she burst out crying. I remember thinking, *What on earth is she crying for?* After a while, the soldiers had finished the nasi goreng and were done smoking, so they left.

They took the machine guns and loaded them in the sidecars of their motorbikes and drove away over the bridge with loud explosions that sounded like gunfire, but it was just the backfiring of the motorcycles. The rest of the day was just a blur.

The second day of the war still saw excitement. Scores of German planes kept on flying by, and the Dutch antiaircraft artillery kept on firing at them. One German aircraft was hit, and it came down. The pilot was killed when his parachute did not open.

Evacuation

The progress of the German Army was slower than they had anticipated after four days of war because the resistance of the Dutch soldiers was fierce even though their weaponry was poor compared to the German material and went back at least half a century. Nevertheless, the advance of the Germans proceeded relentlessly, and apparently the mayor feared that the route of the invading Nazi troops might go right through Gorkum. Therefore on May 14, he ordered for the entire civilian population of the city to evacuate, apparently without any discussion with the military authorities. In retrospect, it seemed at the very least to have been a questionable decision. It was a lot more dangerous to expose several thousands of people to the dangers of traveling on exposed roads, with German fighter planes overhead strafing everything that moved. Most people would have thought it safer to just stay at home.

While our car was being readied, the bells of all the churches were ringing and booming. The car was loaded up with the whole family—Dad driving, Mom in the passenger seat with the youngest, Pim, on her lap, and the other three brothers in the back. It was a large American-model car, if I remember well, perhaps a Chevrolet. We had to drive across the bridge over the harbor close to our house, then along the harbor because traffic had been diverted to one-way traffic to accommodate the people fleeing the city. I recall the rays of the sun bouncing back from little waves in the water of the Linge harbor. There were only a few because there was almost no wind. We passed our old house on the Havendijk and then took a left again across another bridge and down the Walsteeg toward the Arkel city gate. From there, the road went more or less straight to the north. The streets were more and more crowded with people, the closer we came to the gate. They were packed in, man to man. All cars leaving the city were supposed to be loaded full with passengers, but I did not see any other cars, other than ours, which was not unusual in those days. Although, there were a few horse-drawn wagons chock-full of people. There was plenty to see. Many people were pushing bicycles loaded up with as many of their belongings as they could possibly manage—stacks of clothing and blankets piled up on the handlebars and suitcases or bags on the back. I saw one man who improvised a helmet by putting an iron pot on his head with ropes going from the handles of the pot to his neck to keep it in place. Others had their possessions loaded in baby carriages. Some carried a cat or a birdcage with a canary bird in it or had dogs on a leash. I saw an old lady sitting on top of the tricycle ice-cream cart of a street vendor. Her legs went down in the holes where normally the ice- cream containers were kept. She had a cat on her lap. Police were here and there, posted along the side of the road, urging people to hurry up. It was amazing that in a few hours, a city of twelve thousand people was emptied out, except for a small number of older and ill individuals, who were unable to do any significant walking, and a small detachment of soldiers who had to stay. Once we reached the Arkeldijk, the crowds were slowly thinning out because we in the car could move faster than the people who had to walk, carrying their scarce belongings. The dike was lined on both sides with tall old linden trees. They were clothed in their Easter best with brand-new bright-green spring leaves. This canopy screened us from the German planes with howling engines flying over us on and off, and fortunately, we were not shot at or bombed. We passed small groups of soldiers along the dike who yelled at my dad to stop the car and to camouflage it, presumably with branches from bushes at the edge of the road. My mother told my dad to keep on going and that camouflaging the car was a stupid idea. After all, who had ever seen a square green bush coming down the road? We passed the village of Meerkerk, where people along the road offered water and food, but we kept on going. Later we heard that the military had canceled the mayor's order and started stopping all traffic there and turning everybody around to go back home; all those people on the road were hindering the military withdrawal. But we were already past that point. We must have been some fifteen kilometers from Gorkum when my youngest brother, Pim, became carsick and had to puke. Dad stopped the car on the berm, and Pim did his thing. My mom said, "We should get off the road and find a place to stay somewhere. This whole evacuation is ridiculous anyway. It is more dangerous here on the road than at home."

We stopped at a farm in Lexmond, and the family living there was very gracious and made us feel very welcome. In addition to farming, they had a business repairing wagons, plows, and the like. They fed us lunch with thick cheese sandwiches and had us drink milk, which was straight from the cow. Dad had to go back to Gorkum because he had several chronic patients in town who could not be evacuated, and if there was any fighting, wounded people could be expected. In the meantime, we had great fun running around the pastures and the orchards. I remember the cherry orchards in clouds of full pink bloom. The sons of the farmer were some ten years older than us and were happy to show us the farm and its equipment. Eventually they made us wooden swords from branches, and we had sword fights. Then Dad returned with the news that the evacuation had been canceled. We had looked forward to sleeping in the hayloft, but going home was even better.

On the same day that Gorkum was being evacuated, Rotterdam—about forty kilometer northwest of Gorkum—saw very heavy fighting with the Dutch marines continuing to deny the German troops access to the bridges over the Maas River. This prevented them from reaching the western parts of the country where most of the Dutch government was located. The German command decided to break the impasse by bombing Rotterdam's center, the older part of the city, where the bridges were located. Some eight hundred people were killed, and the city center was mostly destroyed. Some men in Gorkum claimed that the dark-gray and black clouds that day came from the burning city. I found that difficult to believe. After all, in my eyes, Rotterdam was very far away; but it was probably true.

My mother had a few difficult days because one of her sisters, with her family, lived in Rotterdam. Fortunately, to her great relief we heard in a few days the good news that they were not harmed.

May 15

One of the ways to protect the western area, where the government was located, from an invader from the east had been the *waterlinie*, which basically consisted of inundating large stretches of land with water. The western part of Holland, or the Netherlands (officially), is below sea level. The land was created by surrounding some part of the sea with a dike and then pumping the water out with windmills. As they say, God created the world, but the Dutch created Holland. It was easy to revert the pumping by opening the sluices. There were fortifications, bunkers, and some cities, such as Gorinchem, associated with the *waterlinie*, strengthening the defensive positions. As one could have expected in the era of flying, the airplanes flew right over to drop paratroopers and bombs on the Dutch troops in the west. I could see the water outside the dike covering the Dalem veld. It really was an outmoded and silly idea, almost medieval.

The commander-in-chief decided that further fighting would not make sense and would only lead to destruction of other major cities in Holland, such as Amsterdam and The Hague because the Germans threatened to bomb other big cities. The Dutch army commander ordered capitulation on May 15, 1940. In the meantime, the Dutch government, including the queen and the royal family, had escaped to Great Britain.

The city of Den Helder—where for centuries the Zwaan family and the family of my mother, the De Koks, had lived and which had been the main Dutch navy port, now became a German navy port, where warships were supplied and repaired—became a target of the Royal British Air Force. The city was bombed every night and day (there were some hundred raids) throughout a few months after the capitulation, and because there was no such thing as precision bombing in those days, the bombs meant for the navy wharfs more often hit civilian housing than their intended targets and killed around five hundred Dutch citizens. My grandfather Opa de Kok and two of my mother's sisters lived in Den Helder. One day in June, I saw my mother crying on the phone. She had just gotten the message that one of her sisters, our aunt Nellie Kramer-de Kok, had been killed by British bombs along with her entire family— husband and four children (my cousins).

Fig. 1-1: My aunt Nelie, a sister of my mother with her family.
All six were killed 16 June 1940 by a single British bomb

CHAPTER TWO

Gorinchem, My Birthplace

Fig 2-1: Gorinchem seen from the Merwede river some two centuries ago

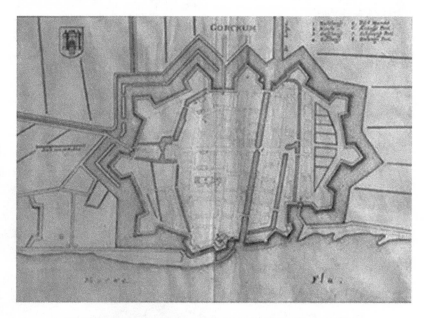

*Fig.2-2: The plan of the walls around old Gorinchem. They
are stil large intact today. The narrow ribbon going vertically
through the middle of the map is the Linge river. At the top it
connects with the canals, that form the outer ring of defense
around the city wall.*

Fig. 2-3: The Great Tower, some five centuries old domineers the old city.

GORINCHEM (GORKUM FOR short) is an old city. Around 1250, it became the property of the lords of Van Arkel. However, it is likely that there was some settlement in the area centuries earlier. The large river, Merwede, ran on the south side on its way to the Rhine Delta, and the much smaller Linge River ran right through the center of the settlement to join the Merwede. The ground must have been quite fertile with frequent inundations by the rivers and must have been good for agriculture, and of course, the terrain and the water were ideal for hunting and fishing. In 1322, the town was granted city rights by Lord Otto van Arkel. Earthen walls and wooden palisades were built around the town for protection, not a luxury, because of the frequent wars between the local lords and counts. Eventually this led to the annexation of Gorkum by the province of Holland in 1417, which resulted in more trade, to the city's benefit. The next century saw the outbreak of the Eighty Years War, a fight for religious freedom and for the independence of Holland from Spain. It was a nasty war causing tens of thousands of casualties. A gruesome example happened in Gorkum when the Geuzen conquered it. They were rebels fighting against the Spanish army that was occupying Holland in the name of the Spanish king.

When I went to sixth grade of elementary school (the School with the Bible) some eighty years ago, I was taught then that the Geuzen—who traveled around Holland with a fleet of small ships—were liberators and heroes, but we were never told about their bestial behavior in Gorkum in 1572. They rounded up all Catholic priests and monks, a total of eighteen. When they refused to switch their belief and become Protestants, they loaded them on their boats and took them to Brielle, some forty kilometers downstream, and tortured them. They disemboweled them, castrated them, burned them, broke their bones, and finally hanged all of them—whether they were dead or alive. After I read about this many years later, in my mind, they became bloodthirsty and murderous thugs rather than heroes. Later these priests and monks were sanctified and are now known as the Martyrs of Gorkum. After many years of negotiation, Holland became an independent and free country in 1642.

The walls around Gorinchem had deteriorated and partly fallen down over the years, and it was decided to rebuild them. At the same time, they were placed farther away from the city center, just about doubling the ground inside the walls. The five-pointed star-shaped system of very high earthen walls, stone walls, bastions, and waterworks is still largely intact although three of the four gates had to be removed in the nineteenth century to accommodate the needs of growing traffic. Near the Waterpoort and the Merwede River and just inside the walls, there was a castle-like building dating from 1598, the Tolkazerne. It was the building where ships had to pay toll before they could navigate the Merwede River. When tolls were no longer required, the Tolkazerne was used for various purposes. When I was a kid, it was used as a public library, and I was a heavy reader of books from *Dr. Doolittle* to Norman Mailer's *The Naked and the Dead* and anything in between. The librarian fortunately let me borrow anything I wanted although some of it was probably not so suited for a thirteen- or fourteen-year-old. Next to the tollhouse was a pond, and it was said that a castle had existed there a long time ago. The legend says that the lady of the castle was not very nice. She refused to give a homeless old man a bit of milk and then had her maids scrub the floors of the castle with milk. The entire castle with everything in and on it sunk into the ground, and only a deep hole remained. This was quickly filled up with water and became a pond, the *duivels gracht* (the devils' pond).

There is a walking path on top of the walls allowing one to walk all the way around the city. When the French troops had to retreat from Holland at the end of the Napoleonic era in 1814, they settled in Gorinchem, and it took a three-month siege to get them out, during which Gorkum was heavily damaged, including the old church going back some four centuries. That was the last fighting until the German occupation.

When I lived in Gorkum, it was still small, having some twelve to thirteen thousand people, but it had expanded outside the city walls with settlements that were built at the expense of the farmland around the city. A few farms inside the city walls were the first to go. This process has continued until today, and now there are around thirty-six thousand inhabitants, of which only a small portion lives inside the city walls. Although there were a number of factories and a wharf building ships, agriculture still constituted a large portion of the economy, and most Mondays, there were three markets. In the space around and between the old Great Church and the city hall, a general market was (and still is) set up, and the merchants exhibited a large variety of their wares in their stalls. Fruit and vegetables, cheese, baked fish, cookies, candy, and of course, Dutch drop (licorice), books and magazines, clothing, shoes, and a great deal more were for sale. Clients came from far and wide. The Great Tower was built in the fifteenth century, but the adjacent church was younger. The Great Church (the St. Maarten's Church) built with the tower, got heavily damaged in 1814 at the end of the Napoleonic period when the retreating French occupied Gorinchem. It had to be demolished, and it was replaced with a new Great Church. It was dedicated in 1851. The tower, which was not damaged, is sixty-seven meters high and can be seen from many kilometers away. It leans a bit, but not as bad as the Tower of Pisa. When I would come home from Amsterdam as a student, usually with the bus, as soon as I saw the tower, I felt I was home.

There were two more markets—one for pigs and one for cows. The pig market was held at the appropriately named Varkensmarkt (*pigs* are called *varkens* in Dutch). The marketplace was divided in squares of about three-by- three yards. Wooden enclosures were placed on each square with the corner poles in holes in the ground to fix them. Several cafés were close by to provide the negotiating farmers with coffee, beer, or something stronger, such as *jenever* (Dutch gin). The Varkensmarkt during the rest of the week was a nice quiet place under the trees, where you could sit on a terrace outside. But on Mondays, the noise was earsplitting; pigs were screaming loudly. Of course, they always scream, but particularly when they got rings attached through their noses. I felt sorry for them. The farmers were bargaining loudly, and with each change in amount, they clapped each other's hands until they agreed. Cows had their own market in the Haarstraat, where a strong rope was installed in the middle of the street, and cows were tied to it. Toward noon, the markets petered out; and by one o'clock, it was pretty much done, leaving it to the city workers to clean up the mess people and beasts left behind, until the next Monday. I believe that a short time after the capitulation, the markets had to be canceled, probably because the Germans "requested" (stole) more and more animals and travel became increasingly dangerous. The general market returned after the war, the cattle and pigs only temporarily.

After the Dutch Capitulation

At first, things appeared rather quickly to return to normal. There were few or no German soldiers around yet; that came later. But fairly soon, more troops started arriving; and their companies marched through Gorkum while singing "Hort, wir fahren, gegen Engeland" (Listen up, we will sail for England), to which we would softly add, "Splash, splash." Most of the German soldiers at this time were behaving decently, sometimes even giving us *kuch* (sourdough bread) or something else to eat. But that was to change soon.

I went to school for the first time in September, the School with the Bible, located at the Kalkhaven. This was previously a harbor, which had been filled in and altered in a space with houses on each long side with trees in front and a terrain in the middle where we could play on breaks. On the opposite side of this terrain was the public school. My age of five years was too young (required age was six years) to go to school, but an exception was made. School was strictly disciplined. The desks were arranged in three neat rows, and when the principal would come in, we all had to stand up next to the left side of our desks until we got permission to sit down. The day started with Bible reading and singing of a religious song and then came the three R's (reading, 'riting and 'rithmetic), history, geography, and so on. There was no talking during lessons. And you better pay attention to the teacher and listen, or you had to stick your hand out and got hit with a ruler. Reading was taught with a tablet that had about twenty pictures on it and a word under the pictures. You had to fish the right letters out of a little box and match them to the word under the picture. The whole class would say together the words out loud until we all knew them by head. The same was done with the numbers. It was an educational system based on learning by rote. There were some interesting (and often fun) interruptions.

One day, our teacher hit a student—let's call him Piet—and sent him to the principal's office. Instead, Piet apparently had gone home. Some ten minutes later, the class door opened. Piet's father marched in, went to the front of the class, grabbed the teacher by his ear, and pulled him the way toward the classroom door, all the while talking, "I will teach you for hitting my son. I am taking *you* to the principal." The entire class was dead silent, and I believe I had my mouth open. I often brought my guinea pigs to school inside my shirt, but once they started whistling very loudly and that was the end of it.

As the war progressed, many articles, such as soap and shampoo, became scarce or were no longer available; and hygiene suffered. Pinworms, fleas, and lice became more prevalent among the students. Our mother would check our hair very carefully with a fine-toothed comb when we would come home from school. We all had an inkwell in the center of our desks. We had to dip our pens in the well to write. Nobody had a fountain pen, and ballpoints did not exist yet. The girl sitting at the desk before me had gorgeous blond hair. It was long and was hanging over my desk. It was heavily populated with little moving critters, lice, and they were falling on my desk. I had great fun picking them up with my pen and drowning them in the inkwell. In the USA, they were known as *cooties*—a word that goes back to WWI when the soldiers fighting in the Flanders trenches got infested with them. In the 1920s, there were even cootie games.

The classrooms were individually heated with large black stoves fed with coal. Obviously the top got quite hot, and it was interesting to place a rubber eraser on the top, as long as the teacher would not see you do it. It would spatter, burn, and smoke—stinking up the place. I may have been suspected, but I never got caught.

In a few words, nothing unusual happened with us in those first two years. That did not hold for others, such as the Jews, who unbeknownst to us kids, feared for their future under the German regime.

CHAPTER THREE

The Jews of Gorinchem

Fig 3-1: The gate and door of the old Gorinchem synagogue.

Fig 3-2: The old Gorinchem synagogue, no longer in existence

SOME OLD DOCUMENTS show that there were already Jews in Gorkum in the thirteenth century, although they were not readily accepted. During a four-year-lasting pest epidemic starting in 1348, people were desperate and large groups of flagellants formed and traveled from town to town, all the while whipping themselves until they were bleeding, in the hope of forgiveness for their sins and of salvation by a Higher Being. Their fear was understandable as in many places, only some 10 percent of the population survived; and of course, there was absolutely no knowledge of the true causes of the disease—the microorganism *Pasteurella pestis*, fleas and rats that spread it around, and very poor hygiene. The flagellants also reached Gorkum, and eight houses with people in them were burned. Although it was not mentioned, the families in the houses were most likely Jewish.

In later years, Holland became much more tolerant. For instance, in 1796, the Council of the Bataafse Republic (the Dutch government) came to the conclusion that "no Jew may be excluded from any rights or advantages that are attached to the Bataafs citizenship." Gorkum was ahead of the country government as a whole by a hundred years and announced a similar rule in 1696. Any Jew could become a full citizen by taking the oath for the Jewish citizen. Clear evidence that this was not just an empty promise was an event in 1767 when four non-Jewish butchers requested from the mayor that Jewish butchers no longer should be admitted to the city or to the guild, obviously to reduce competition. Good butchers were often Jews because of the religious requirements for kosher butchery. The request was turned down, and Jews were free to practice their trade. The number of Jews in Gorinchem grew, and with that, the need for a synagogue grew. First, a few smaller buildings were rented until enough money was collected, interestingly, with contributions from the city and province government. Construction of a new synagogue began in 1841 and, after completion, was formally dedicated by a rabbi who traveled down from Rotterdam. A number of smaller structures, such as a classroom and a ritual bath (mikvah), were added later. Needless to say, all of these required significant expenses, partially paid for by loans. In 1851, these had not entirely been paid off. King William III helped with a gift of one hundred guilders—a large sum of money at that time. The Jews lived freely in Gorkum and, to an extent, mingled with the general population; but their numbers shrunk, mostly because of the departure to larger cities such as Amsterdam, which had a relatively large Jewish population and offered more chance for a Jewish marriage and for appropriate work. Assimilation played a smaller role.

The German takeover was feared by many, Jewish or not. The events in Germany were not encouraging, but initially the Krauts behaved correctly in Gorinchem. Worse things to come were unavoidable. The Jewish Mr. Nort was an optician with his business in the center of Gorkum. His relatives in Germany kept him informed about the terrible way the Jews were treated, such as Kristallnacht. After the Dutch capitulation and the German takeover, he was filled with fear for the future. He killed his three kids, his wife, and then himself. This may have been an extremely drastic step but, in view of later developments, it was understandable. The noose around the Jewish necks was loose but started to be tightened. On July 31, a rule was announced that forbade kosher slaughter. This really affected Orthodox Jews. Next, no new Jewish government employees could be hired; and shortly later, those that already worked for the government were fired. The Jewish midwife and the man teaching Hebrew at the Latin school Gymnasium Camphusianum had to go. Many others were fired. Corporations had to report Jewish stockholders. Three of the five family physicians in Gorkum could only see Jewish patients because they were Jews themselves. That was a difficult problem for the delivery of health care. There were only two non-Jewish family physicians. Funds over ten thousand guilders, stocks, and savings accounts owned by Jews had to be transferred to the Lippman et al. Banking Firm in Amsterdam. From there, I am certain, that all the funds disappeared in the pot of the Deutsche Reich. Signs saying "Forbidden for Jews" appeared on theaters, libraries, swimming pools, and multiple other institutions, such as cafés and restaurants. Bicycles and radios belonging to Jews had to be turned in to the mayor's office. My father had many Jewish patients. He ignored the rules and continued seeing them, and at times, my brothers and I accompanied him. He usually used his bicycle, and I or one of my brothers would sit on the luggage carrier in the back. A Jewish family I really liked to visit was the Feilchenfelds. They had fled from Germany when the Nazis came to power and settled in Gorkum. They had a second-floor apartment above a carpenter's workshop on the Langendijk, half a block from our home. The husband was in his mid-seventies and was kind of quiet. He loved to read and had many books and cartoon collections, all in German and some maybe in Yiddish, but I would not have recognized that. His wife was about fifteen years younger. She was lively and nice and had stories to tell about what it was like in old Germany before Hitler came to power. She always had a candy or a cookie for me.

Fig. 3-3 : Mrs. Feilchenfeld on the right, with a grandchild and
a companion. She immigrated to the U.S.A. after surviving the
concentration camp Dachau

One day, she was kind of dancing around the dining room table
saying, "When the Germans forget us, we will have a big party and
dance around the table." Of course, the Germans did not; and one
day, Jan, one of my younger brothers, saw them being picked up
on the Langendijk by Dutch (!) policemen, who generally simply
did what the Germans ordered them to do. They were taken to the
railroad station (by taxicab no less) and from there by train to the
concentration camp Bergen-Belsen. Jewish kids could no longer
attend public schools; therefore, a Jewish school was started in
the synagogue with a Jewish teacher. Public and Christian schools
were ordered to report how many Jews were registered with the
school, a rather unlikely event. The only one who refused to his
credit to submit a report was the director of the Christian School
of Education, Mr. Groen, stating that this requirement was against
Christian principles. The noose was tightened in the winter of
1940/41. Vandals broke into the synagogue and did a great deal

of damage. Fortunately, the Torah were not damaged and were
saved. One probable reason for all these measures was to isolate
the Jews from the general public but for certain, not the only one.
The noose was tightened more. Jews, including half- and quarter-
Jews, were mandated to fill out a form with all their information
(birthday, family, employer, address, and so on). This form was to
be handed in to the mayor's office. The list showed 103 full-Jews,
4 quarter-Jews (one Jewish grandparent), and 19 half-Jews (two
Jewish grandparents). Copies of all the registrations were sent to
the German Sicherheitspolizei. About one quarter of the Jews were
noncitizens who had fled from the Nazis and ended up in Gorkum.
Also, from May 1942, all Jews had to wear a David star on their
clothing, a six-pointed yellow star with the word *Jew* on its center.
To add insult to injury, they had to pay for both the registration and
the star. For the last, they also had to hand over one textile coupon
of the ration card. All citizens received an identity card; for Jews,
stamped with a large *J* next to their picture. On January 20, 1942,
the Nazis had a large conference in Wannsee (now infamous),
where they decided on a final solution of the "Jewish" problem. Not
long afterward began the deportations to the "work camps." It was
an easy task because the Krauts had the addresses of everyone from
the registration. The family Van Bueren (husband, wife, and two
children) was the first on August 15, 1942, and by August 31, the
wife and children were already gone, murdered in the gas chambers
of Auschwitz. Their dad, Juda, survived the Holocaust until
December 31, 1943. On the way to my class, I started to see more
empty buildings and shops, often with broken windows or doors
that seemed to have been kicked in. By the end of 1943, only nine
of the deported Jews were still alive. At the end of the war, some
thirty Jews had survived, mostly by going "underground." Very few
survived in the concentration camps. Among them was my friend
Hannah Feilchenfeld. To our great astonishment and gratefulness,
we found out she survived the Holocaust because some months
after the war, we received an aid package with clothing, chocolate,
and some books and magazines from the USA sent by her. She had
changed her name to Hannah Fields. Others had gone underground
and had been able to find a Dutch home or homes where they stayed

until the end of the war. This was quite dangerous for their Dutch hosts. The Nazis threatened severe reprisals, including execution of Jews and Dutch alike, if any Jews were found. Some were betrayed and as yet arrested. This presumably happened to Anna Frank and her family in Amsterdam. But in many years no evidence for the existence of a traitor of Anna and her family has been found. Recent researchers believe that there was no traitor and that their arrest was due to very bad luck. The Dutch resistance played a large role in the rescue efforts to save Jews by finding hiding places and providing the hiding people with ration card coupons stolen from the distribution centers. The coupons were needed to buy food, clothing, and the like. Sometimes the Jews had to be brought from one place to another for safety. My dad played a large role in all this but never talked about it to us, kids, obviously for security reasons, and we had no idea what was going on. He did not tell us even after the war was over. But it must have been considerable because some years after the war, he was recognized by Yad Vashem in Jerusalem and registered as a Righteous Among the Nations.

Fig. 3-4: I.D. cards became mandatory in 1941. The ones for Jews were marked with a large capital J

When the war was over and with the so diminished number of Jews (the census in 1947 counted only twenty-eight), it became too expensive and indeed impossible to maintain the synagogue, so it was sold to the city. With renewal plans for the neighborhood where the synagogue was located, it was demolished in 1955. The wind vane and three of the cornerstones from the front wall, all with the Jewish number 5601 for the year 1841, are now in the Gorkums Museum.

Part of this chapter is based on what I remember, but as a five- to eight- year-old kid with parents who tried to shield me from the awful events associated with the Nazi regime, there are many hiatus in my memories. I have tried to fill these by studying a number of books about the war and by talking with survivors of the war. The following book was particularly helpful: *Joods Gorinchem* by B. Stamkot et al. (1989). After the war I gradually learned that some 60,000,000 people had lost their lives in the war, and that the Nazis were responsible for the murdering of at least 6,000,000 Jews and millions more with the most ghastly methods. I could not understand, that an Almighty and Benevolent God could allow it all to happen. I began to doubt that He or She really existed.

CHAPTER FOUR

The Physicians' Resistance

IT WAS FALL and was getting colder every day. Air-raid alarms became more frequent. The year before the Germans had started to try to transform the Koninklijke Nederlandse Vereniging voor Bevordering van de Geneeskunde (the equivalent of the AMA) into an organization that was pro-German, the Artsen Kamer (comparable to the German Artzenkammer), its goal being to control the policies of the organization with regard to the Jewish population, euthanasia of handicapped individuals and other Nazification measures. When they had no success because of a lack of cooperation by the Dutch physicians, they closed down the Dutch AMA and replaced it with the Artsen Kamer anyway. I believe they also published a number of regulations about reporting Jewish patients to the authorities. This stimulated massive resistance by the Dutch physicians, of which some 6,200 (more than 95 percent) returned their medical organization's memberships to the authorities. They still had their medical licenses anyway and were still able to practice medicine even without the membership. A number even closed their practices. This forced the German authorities to accept a compromise. My father and one other physician, the surgeon Dr. de Roos from our town, were the only physicians, who had refused to sign the so-called Jewish declaration in addition to not becoming members of the German-mandated medical organization. This, in essence, would have been a statement of allegiance to the occupying authorities. My dad, who was a family physician in our small town of Gorinchem, had received a summons in the summer to appear at the *ortskommandantur* in Rotterdam (the regional German headquarters) for civil disobedience, as had his colleague,

27

the surgeon. They departed for Rotterdam, fully expecting to be back in a few hours. When they did not return, my mother, who was several months pregnant, became very worried and talked a friend into driving her to the German headquarters in Rotterdam. There she found out that the two doctors had been found guilty and sentenced to three months of prison and were about to be put on a train full of prisoners bound for the concentration camp in Amersfoort. Probably because she was visibly pregnant (the Germans were all in favor of propagation of the race), she was given a few minutes to say goodbye. Dad survived and came back three months later—skinny as a rat, bald with all his hair cut off, and well-tanned from working outside, chopping rocks. He never wanted to talk about his experiences, which—I am sure— must have been horrible. He did once tell me that Camp Amersfoort had three divisions—first for ordinary criminals; second, a transit area for Jews about to be shipped to Germany; and third for political prisoners, such as my dad and typical for my dad, that was all he ever said about it. My brother Jan remembered a story he heard from our dad. After the war, Fort Vuren—an old part of the *waterlinie*— was used to lock up traitors, collaborators with the Germans, black marketeers, and others. Dad was appointed as camp physician. One day, Jan accompanied him and waited in a long corridor until Dad was done. The prisoners were allowed to be out of their cells and to pass the time in the corridor. He saw one small man, who was making wooden toys, and Jan talked with him for a while until they got into the car to return home. Jan said, "I really don't think it is fair that nice guy is locked up."

Dad said, "Let me tell you something. When I was a prisoner in Amersfoort, I saw with my own eyes your nice little man beating several people to death."

The day after Dad's return, he went straight back to seeing patients, some in the office but most by house calls, done on the bike or on a motorcycle. Our life returned to relative normality.

CHAPTER FIVE

1943–1944

Fig 5-1 : The family in the garden of Eind 14, early in 1943.

Fig. 5-2: The four brothers on dad's motor cycle.

Illness

AS A WHOLE, we were remarkably healthy despite lack of vitamins and the like and despite some food shortages. Our mother had been able to get some bottles of cod liver oil, and during wintertime, we were all lined up at night to swallow a teaspoonful of the stuff. It tasted awful. Afterward, we were awarded with a bit of sugar to get rid of the taste. I do remember that when my dad showed up with his syringes and needles to give us our vaccinations, we flew as chaff in the wind in all directions, looking for a hiding place. He had a silver-colored, about ten-to-twelve-centimeter-long cylinder filled with alcohol—holding his syringe and the needles—and a cap that was screwed on top. He carried it always in the pocket of his jacket. Of course, that meant that he was prepared to give injections at any time. Dad was insulted when we ran and hid because he saw it as a sign that we did not trust him, as he told us that it would not hurt. I do not know if we eventually got the required shots because I do not remember. My brother Jan got quite ill that spring, probably not because of a lack of vaccinations because none of the other kids got sick. He was isolated in one room, and it looked as if he was not going to make it. A consultant came from Utrecht—a professor of the medical faculty—and recommended a blood transfusion, which was donated by Corrie, our cousin. I am not sure if it was tested for compatibility or if my dad just gambled that the blood would cause no problems as the donor and the patient were related. Corrie worked for Dad as a physician assistant and lived with us. To this day, I have no idea what disease Jan had, but luckily he slowly got better.

Thieves

Holland had been occupied by the Germans for three and a half years. Life became more difficult, and many articles became scarce. Even the ration coupons did not help much because there was little or nothing available. My mother had a capable seamstress who lived closely by. She made some clothing for us from horse blankets. It looked weird. Worse, it itched like crazy. Then disaster struck when our house got broken into. Burglars came to the house probably with a small rowboat through the harbor because there was a nighttime curfew. On the water, they were much less visible. They broke into our house by lifting a glass-in-lead panel from one of the windows next to the front door. They got in the hall where all our heavy coats and other winter clothing were hanging and stole the whole lot. It was a disaster. The only one who still had his winter coat and his gloves was my brother Jan, who was a bit sloppy. He did not hang up his winter coat, and he stored it by throwing it under his bed. Having the coats and so on disappear caused a major problem because after several years of war, everything was scarce, particularly textiles. You needed ration coupons to get any textiles, and if replacements were available at all, you were very lucky. To make things worse, the oncoming winter was expected to be harsh. To the relief of my parents, friends and patients who heard of our ordeal fortunately donated enough to see us through. My parents, my brothers, and I did not have to freeze even though a really cold winter was expected. One piece of clothing all of us absolutely refused to wear, no matter how cold it was outside, was a donated khaki coat because we were not going to be seen with a "pig farmer's coat." After we were liberated, our smart mother had it made into a jacket similar to an allied army jacket, and we fought over it.

Christmas Present 1943

My brothers and I knew that we would have a new family member pretty soon, and we decided that only a boy would do; a girl would be sent back to where she came from. Obviously the whole process of birth was a mystery to us. Christmas was coming closer, but we did not count on any gifts. Even Santa Claus would not be able to find many or any presents, but we did have a decorated Christmas tree. Early on Christmas morning, we ran downstairs to look under the tree, and miraculously there were a few presents. Our parents were still in bed. When we went to their bedroom to tell them, we heard a baby crying! Dad, just home on time from the concentration camp, had delivered our new sister around two in the morning. My parents were very happy, finally having a girl after four boys. Our plans for "no girls in the house" were quickly forgotten. My dad was so excited that he went out to call the florist, one of his patients, out of bed at 3:00 a.m. to get flowers for my mother. Of course, none were available, and he had to settle for a Christmas wreath, which he used to decorate my parents' bedroom. My parents named the baby Irene, meaning "peace," wishing for rapid peace even though the worst was still to come in the next eighteen months of war.

Treasure Hunt

It was late in 1943, and Holland had been occupied by the Nazis for three- plus years. More and more bombers were flying over on their way to Germany, apparently following the Rhine to their targets. I was glad to see them because the more the Nazis got punished, the better. Typically for my brother Kees, he was sad to see them because he felt sorry for the German women and children. Our parents were gone for a day to visit family members in Amsterdam, and my brothers found a hidden trapdoor on the second floor of our home in our small town. It was hidden under a large old blanket chest. When it was lifted, we saw a hole, which was deep enough for an adult to stand upright in; and it appeared to extend for several yards. The house was old, and the space was between two floors next to the area of the kitchen chimney. Of course, we all climbed in and, to our great surprise and delight, found a treasure of silver and gold dinnerware, silver vases, jewelry, and so on. There was also a radio. We just knew that this had to have been left behind by pirates, hidden while they were escaping, never to return. We proceeded to take it all out and decorated our parents' bedroom with the loot. Needless to say, our parents were rather surprised when they saw all the decorations. They were also aghast because the "pirate" treasure really belonged to Jewish families who had gone underground. My parents were hiding it for them. The treasure went fast back into its hiding place. We were sworn to secrecy, not just about the treasure, but particularly about the radio. The Germans had long ago confiscated all radios, and when caught with a radio in one's possession, you had a good chance to promptly be executed. My dad would crawl into the treasure hole and listen with the clandestine radio to the BBC to keep track of the progress of the war. There was a division, Radio Orange, which broadcasted in Dutch. It also sent signals in code for the Dutch resistance. Every so often, I would listen with him, and I remember particularly some speeches of Winston Churchill. I did not know any English, and being around eight years old, I probably would not have understood the meaning of his words anyway. But there was something very reassuring about his sonorous voice, a conviction that the bad times would pass and that all would be well. This was about seventy-five years ago, and it has stayed with me for all that time.

Fights and Riots

Fig.5-3:The kids outside the windows watching the turmoil in the street

On several occasions, fights broke out between NSBers trying to sell their Nazi newspapers, favorable to the German occupiers, on the streets of Gorkum. This led inevitably to discussions with bypassing citizens. The NSBers were sometimes accompanied by the WA for protection. They were the military arm of the NSB, and they marched around in black uniforms with heavy leather belts. One day, my brothers and I were in our living room looking out. It was a perfect spot because our living quarters were on top of the floor of our dad's practice, so we had a great view over the entire Eind. It was like having the best seats in a theater. We could see a riot developing, first the discussions but with more and more people getting involved; fists started flying. Some German soldiers entered the melee; and the leader of the WA, his face all red, started to yell, "Onward, men of the WA, beat them up." The WA men took their leather belts and started swinging them around. It was quite a spectacle, but finally, the police came and restored order. On another occasion, it was the birthday of Prince Bernhard, the husband of Princess Juliana, and many people wore a white carnation, the favorite flower of the prince. German soldiers considered this a provocation and pulled them off jackets and dresses, roughing the wearers up in the process. A telephone wire connecting the quarters of the commander of engineer troops to the telephone center was found broken, and the Germans suspected sabotage. The Krauts declared a curfew for teenagers up to age twenty-one between 7:00 p.m. and 7:00 a.m. In addition, two-men teams of adults had to stand guard throughout the night at various points in the city that the Germans considered vulnerable. New teams rotated every two hours. This constituted quite a burden for a large number of citizens who had been placed on the guard list. It was generally considered as punishment by the *ortscommandant*, who was unhappy with the *deutsch-feindliche* (hostile to Germans) attitude of many Gorkumers.

As a physician, who often had to take care of patients at night, dad was exempt from the guard duty.

German Labor Problems

Although the German troops had been quite successful in over three years of war—with a large portion of Western Europe and Poland and most of the Baltic countries in the East now in German's hands—the cost was high, and they lost literally several hundred thousands of casualties. Many additional men were called up to replace the fallen and had to leave the factories and the farms with consequential shortages of workers and, obviously, industrial and agricultural products. Several solutions were tried. First voluntary service from the workers in the occupied countries was initiated by setting up an *Arbeits Dienst* (labor service). Not surprisingly, this was not exactly a success because very few people were interested in volunteering to go to Germany to work. Secondly, prisoners of the concentration camps, some of whom were still strong enough and able to work, were utilized in industries close to the camps. For instance, the production of the V-1 and V-2 rockets at the Peenemünde base at the Baltic Sea, which took some 350 hours of labor for one rocket, was entirely dependent on the fifteen to twenty thousand slave laborers from the neighboring concentration camp. When the recruiting of voluntary workers was a failure, mandatory service became unavoidable. So the steel factory of De Vries Robbé in Gorinchem had to deliver 120 workers, and those were well trained. This happened all over the place, and in the southern part of the province of Zuid-Holland, several thousand workers were transported to Germany for forced labor. The Germans also stopped people— of what they considered a work-capable age of eighteen to fifty-one years— in the street, arrested them, and put them on the train to Germany unless they had an *ausweis*, a form that excused them. The conditions for getting an

ausweis were continually strengthened. For instance, teachers initially were free from the service in Germany, but later their *ausweisen* became invalid. To avoid being sent to Germany, many teachers went underground. With a lack of teachers and of fuel to warm the schools, they had to close. After 1943, political prisoners, such as my dad had been, were also shipped to Germany to help maintain the German war machine.

On October 3, 1944 at 8:00 p.m., all sirens of the air-raid alarm system started howling. There was no air raid and no airplane anywhere in sight. In retrospect, it was clear that the noise was meant to keep everybody inside at home and to mask a large-scale razzia that was about to begin. It also was a sign for the involved troops to begin the razzia. Soldiers from the Wehrmacht and the Waffen SS went in small groups to specific houses. They had a list with names and addresses. The previous afternoon, some of the troops had gone around in Gorinchem for a reconnaissance of the intended targets. As soon as the sirens started, the soldiers knocked on the doors of the house that was assigned to them and asked for specific persons; and if they were not home, they would search the house. For instance, the sons of the family Sommer had stayed upstairs when the Germans came. They climbed on the roof through a roof window as soon as the soldiers knocked on their housedoor. They were lying flat on the roof with their feet against the chimney to avoid being seen and sliding down. After a short while, someone ticked on the window to indicate that the Germans were gone. When they climbed back in the attic, they heard that the soldiers had taken their father with them when they could not find the two sons. In the morning, they went to prearranged hiding places. One went to neighbors; the other stayed at home in a hollowed-out organ. Some hundred young Gorkumers had been arrested, and all of them were kept in a previous old sugar factory Hollandia under German guards. A lady came by the house with a message from their father with a warning: "Stay away from here. This does not look good." Later they found out that their dad was brought from the improvised prison to another building for a medical exam because he had stomach bleeding. During the transport, he got a chance to write the warning; and he just dropped it on the road, where a woman found it and brought it to the Sommers' home. When his medical problem was confirmed, he was discharged and got to go home. There were 102 remaining prisoners. They were transported to Amersfoort, and there they were divided in two groups by alphabet, A to Kr and Kr to Z. Another large group of prisoners came from

Putten. This was a small town in Gelderland, one of the eleven Dutch provinces.

On October 1, 1944, a small number of men from the Dutch resistance ambushed a German army vehicle with four Germans: two were officers, and two were corporals. Three were wounded, and one officer died a day later from his wounds. One of the Dutchmen also died. Revenge was unavoidable. The next day, German troops surrounded Putten—the town closest to the site of the attack on the German car—to prevent anyone from escaping. Six hundred sixty men from sixteen years of age and up were arrested, while the women were rounded up and locked in the church. Fortunately, the women were later released, and the church was not burned as what happened in some other locations. But well over a hundred houses were burned down. Fifty- nine of the men were released because of having a handicap or being aged. This left 602 prisoners who were shipped to Amersfoort, a *Polizeiliches Durchgangs Lager* (Police Transit Camp). The first group from Gorinchem— forty-two men from the razzia plus some additions and all of the Putten prisoners—was shipped to a concentration camp in northwest Germany, Neuengamme. This was one of the worst places to be interned. The men were terribly treated, and only four people of the Gorkum group survived and forty-eight from the Putten men.

The second group of some sixty Gorkumers was sent to Deelen, an airport, to dig ditches. They did well probably because discipline was lax. One man got ill and passed away, but all the others survived. Some were released by the camp administration, while others walked away and just disappeared.

It has never become entirely clear where the list with the names of the arrested men came from. Most belonged to the middle class; most were members of the water polo club Gorinchem or the hockey club Rapid or both. It seems likely that the list was based on a collection of anonymous letters sent to the NSB headquarters or written by members of the NSB, most of whom were blue-collar workers and may have been jealous of the advantages available to the middle class. What may have hurt most was that the sons of the first group had a much larger chance to be sent to Germany for forced labor, while members of the second group were at much less risk to be shipped off and could play their sports. The mayor's office and police department probably put the list of *deutsch feindliche* (hostile to the Germans) Dutch citizens together and eventually handed it over to the German commander.

Hostages

A different group of prisoners was the hostages. They were prominent men and women, imprisoned mostly in the camp at St. Michielsgestel or Camp Vught, where they would readily be available for execution if *represailles* were deemed necessary. Ten prominent people from Gorkum were selected for this purpose. The hostages were not maltreated, but they must have been in constant fear that their time might be up at any moment. My uncle Wim, a brother of my dad, who was a minister of the Dutch Reformed Church, was held as a hostage for a number of months before being released.

Ukrainians

In 1943/44, in many areas, German troops were replaced with Ukrainians— usually referred to as Russians or white Russians— mostly in a combat support role, probably again a reflection of the increasing shortage of German manpower because of the long duration of the war. The Ukrainians had fought the Germans in Russia and were made prisoners of war on the Eastern Front. They were given the choice of signing up with the German army. They hated the Russian government for what Stalin had done to organize the individual Ukrainian farms into large government-controlled cooperatives. Millions of farmers and their families were killed or starved to death. Many of the Ukrainian prisoners of war signed up for the German army rather than to be locked up in the concentration camps or be worked to death as forced laborers. This way, German troops were freed up for the fight. I do not know how many there were in Gorkum, but there might have been enough of them to form a combat support battalion.

We were afraid of them, and many rumors about them made the rounds, such as that they often got drunk on antifreeze and that they hunted and ate cats and dogs. In their free time, they often patrolled around on the city walls. They used their rifles with .22 inserts to hunt the many pigeons in the trees on the walls. They mostly were used for transports. Harvests of wheat grain and sugar beets were confiscated from the farms or stolen from the farmers, loaded on carts and horses, and brought to ships in the harbor to be taken to Germany. Whether any of the ships ever made it up the Rhine, I do not know, but the Allied fighter planes patrolled very actively over the Rhine and fired their board cannons or rockets at everything that moved. At the least, it must have been a rather hazardous journey. For the Dutch, the theft of all these supplies, particularly food, was to have major consequences during the upcoming winter when thousands of Dutchmen died because they had nothing to eat.

Besides food, a great many things became very scarce and difficult to find. Some people profited from the shortages. The house of our neighbor at Het Eind, the widow Witmer, was packed with tools and nails, screws, and so on. Her third floor was so crammed full with storage racks that you hardly could walk between them. Her husband might have been a hoarder. She sold or traded the stuff to farmers and workers who could not find it anywhere else. If we helped her out, she awarded us with an apple, of which she had plenty. She would look through her supply and would come up with the smallest or a half-rotten one.

CHAPTER SIX

Bombs Thrown and Bombs Flown

Fig 6-1: The bombed and sunk ferry Gorinchem V

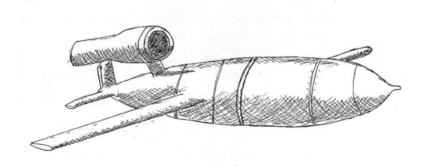

Fig. 6-2: Sketch of a V-1. The engine looked like a stove pipe lying on the rocket.

Machine Guns and Artillery

EVEN BEFORE THE landing of the Allied armies in Normandy on June 6, 1944, the feeling was that the liberation was almost there, but it still took more than a year. It was very clear that the activities in the air increased dramatically. On hearing an air-raid alarm, which became very common, we would run into the house and go to the arched vault, which was the connection between the entry into our semibasement and the location of my dad's practice. This was considered the safest spot in the house. Sometimes things went not quite according to plan. During one air-raid alarm, we all ran into the house with Jan being the last one, but he was locked out when the kid before him slammed the door shut. He still remembers how scared he was standing outside during the air raid. Another time, we were playing Red Cross with one of the neighborhood kids tied to a board used as an improvised stretcher. The air-raid alarm sounded, and we dropped the stretcher as a stone. Later, when the Allied artillery was closer by on the south side of the Merwede River, they could and did shoot grenades across the river almost every night. Their goal probably was Fort Vuren, which was five kilometers to the east from the city, on the north riverbank, and where German troops were quartered. My mom always had one or two teenage girls working with her for training. One of them, a very friendly girl, Niesje, lived with her family in a small home close to the fort. She traveled with her bike some five kilometers, up and down, riding over the dike along the river, in the morning to come to work in our house and in the evening to go home again. One morning, dad told us that Niesje would not be back. She was killed the night before. During an artillery barrage, her neck was cut by a piece of shrapnel, and she bled to death.

It seemed that one reason for the increase in air activity was to cut off all traffic by land or by air to impede the movements of the Germans back to the fatherland. Gorinchem was positioned on probably the most important North–South Axis connecting Antwerp, Brussels, and even Paris with the western part of Holland (where the largest cities were located). From Holland to Germany was a relatively short trip. There was no bridge across the river at the time, but there were two ferries. The first was called the *Janihudi*, a small ship that was meant for pedestrians and bicyclists and maybe a small car. It went upstream to a small town by the name of Woudrichem on the south side of the river. Many kids from Woudrichem used the ferry to go to school in Gorinchem. The other ferry, the *Gorinchem V*, went downstream to Sleeuwijk, also on the south side of the Merwede River, located more or less across from Gorinchem. It was much larger than the other ferry and was capable of transporting a number of vehicles at the same time. Thus, it was important for the retreating German troops.

On March 8, 1944, the air-raid alarms went off. It was about 4:30 p.m., after school. I was with my dad, who was making house calls. I was outside waiting for him to finish up. I saw two fighter planes—later I heard that they were British—coming in over the river from the west. Then they dove down toward the river, and I could see little flames flickering up from their wings and heard the explosions of their board cannons. A few minutes later, they climbed up and flew away in a large arc toward the south. The air-raid alarms went silent. Dad came running from the house and said, "You will have to walk home because I have to go to the hospital right away. They shot up the *Janihudi*." He jumped in his car and was gone. So I walked home; it was not very far. When Dad came home, he looked really sad. He said that not just the *Janihudi* had been machine-gunned but also a few other small ships. All the victims, though, came from the *Janihudi*. There were six dead and twelve wounded. All the dead were kids from the *Janihudi*. One was the older brother of a friend of ours. He lived in Gorkum but decided to accompany his girlfriend on her way home from school. I went to look at the ship, which was tied up just outside the Waterpoort. The ship was full of holes from the bullets, and on the deck were several red puddles of blood, even pieces of human flesh.

Why did they attack a boat full of children going home from school? There were even red crosses painted all over it.

A few months later, the other main ferry with a German crew—who had replaced the Dutch sailors—was attacked, and it sank in the small Sleeuwijk harbor. That cut the last important connection between the north and south sides of the Merwede. There were still a few smaller ships left, but it handicapped the crossing of German military.

Bombs

October and November 1944 were very bad months for Gorinchem. Bombs were falling almost every other day and night. Sometimes the bombs fell very close by. In one attack they hit two targets across from our house on the opposite side of the harbor, some 50 yards away. One fell on Tony's café, a small neighborhood pub, and several hit the ZHB brewery, which was totally destroyed. It was so close that the explosions blew the glass out of most of our windows. The bombs probably were meant for an anti aircraft artillery battery positioned on the city hall. Much later, when I was legally allowed to drink beer, I figured that the pilot of the plane must have been a teetotaler. These air attacks seemed to be planned and were probably related to the advances of the Allied forces toward the Merwede River. Aerial fights were also common. We thought them to be quite spectacular. We'd stand on the bench in the waiting room of my dad and watch it all. Antiaircraft artillery was dug in at many locations on the city walls, and when they were firing, it looked as if strings of Christmas lights were hung up in the air. Little black clouds appeared in the air around the airplanes from the exploding grenades. Sometimes a plane got hit, and you could see the crew jumping out with their parachutes. The Germans would continue firing at the flyers even when they were hanging helplessly in the air. Some courageous Dutchmen would hurry to get to their landing sites ahead of the Germans so that they could smuggle them away to a safe hiding place before they became prisoners of war or were killed. I remember a story being told at one occasion where the Krauts killed a wounded flier, together with the Dutch physician who was helping him with his wounds, by throwing a hand grenade at them. After the sirens announced the end of the air attack with a continuous sound, rather than the varying up and down tones announcing an attack, we would hurry outside to look for souvenirs, such as pieces of shrapnel or spent cartridges from the board weapons, which were attractive because they were made of bright, shiny copper. We had to be careful when picking them up because they, initially, were red-hot. Sometimes the sirens were going for several hours, so we could not go to play outside and had to sleep in the basement. We considered it all as a grand adventure, undoubtedly, because our mother—later aided by her sister, Tante Leen—somehow was able to project an aura of security despite the threats and chaos of war all around us.

(I am writing this on June 6, 2019, seventy-five years after D-day, the greatest invasion the world has ever seen. There were 7,000 ships; 150,000 troops; and 4,000 American and British deaths on the very first day! The courage of the men—who jumped from the landing ships into the sea, sometimes drowning with their heavy equipment, and who stormed the beaches under heavy fire from machine guns, rifles, and artillery salvos—is unimaginable. I can't stop thinking about it today with a sense of awe and gratefulness.)

Dad told us about it and explained that this was the beginning of the end for the Third Reich. He had a map of Europe on which he kept track of the progress of the war with a fat purple marker (maybe a skin marker). Almost every day, he listened to the Dutch division of the BBC for the latest news from the front. The radio and the map were kept hidden in the "treasure place." We were all sworn to secrecy because if the Nazis found out, it could have deadly consequences.

The collateral damage of the bombardments, as usual, outdid the damage afflicted to the Germans by a large margin. Many houses were destroyed, and many inhabitants were killed. Some of the attacks may have been aimed at military targets but worked out otherwise. After the *Gorinchem V* ferry boat had been bombed and sunk, remaining ferries were much smaller, and it took much longer to transport German soldiers and vehicles—withdrawing from the fighting in France and Belgium to strengthen the troops in Germany itself —across the river. When the first troops had crossed, they would wait for the remainder of the convoy to arrive before departing for Germany. To avoid being seen by the Allied fighter planes, they would try to hide in some of the very narrow shopping streets in Gorkum, such as the Kortendijk and Langendijk. This created a major chaos because the streets were clogged with soldiers and vehicles but even more with horses pulling carts. After all, the bulk of the transport of the German armies was on foot or with wagons pulled by horses. The bombardment on November 4 may have been aimed at such a convoy, or maybe it was destined for one of the positions of the antiaircraft on the walls. But a number of houses was hit. One bomb landed on a house on the Havendijk, and it was a good hit because it belonged to the leader of the NSB in Gorkum. It was knocked to smithereens. After he left Gorkum, the house was used as the headquarters of the local NSB. Needless to say, many citizens of Gorkum were quite pleased and thought that the bombing of this house was intentional. But many other houses were also destroyed, so I believed that it was just a lucky shot.

The last bombing took place on January 6, 1945. By mid-1944, another player had appeared on the stage, the V-1. I once took a map of Gorinchem and plotted the locations where bombs had been dropped. The destruction formed a bit of a half circle around our house with a diameter of one hundred to two hundred meters. I guess we were lucky not to be hit, although frequently we would have broken windows.

V-1

The V-1 became operational in the middle of 1944, after almost a decade of development. The letter *V* stands for *Vergeltung* (revenge). It looked like a small airplane with a horizontal stovepipe mounted on top near the tail. The wings and the warhead were made of plywood to reduce the weight. The warhead was stuffed with one thousand kilograms of explosive, and it would go off as soon as it hit the ground. It was powered with a simple pulse-jet engine, which pulsed fifty times per second and produced a characteristic *putputput* noise. The V-1 had a cruising altitude of six hundred to nine hundred meters, which was close enough to the ground that one could hear the sound; hence, the nicknames of Maikåfer (May bug), doodlebug, or buzz bomb. I found them very frightening because we were told that as the *putputput* stopped, the jet would come down. Most of the V-1s were propelled from an inclined launch ramp, similar to the system that launches planes from an aircraft carrier, while fewer were air launched from a plane. After the Allied forces reconquered all of France and advanced through Belgium, the V-1 launching sites from the ground were lost to the Germans and some of the sites were relocated to Twente in northeast Holland. The flight route from Twente to London and later to Antwerp during the Ardennes offensive ran over Gorkum and its environment. The city was never the target of the rockets, but a few did come down in the countryside around Gorkum. To my knowledge, nobody got killed by them in or around my hometown. But one exploded near a body of water, and the enormous pressure change disturbed the air bladder of large numbers of fish, making them float to the surface. When discovered by neighbors, many fishes were scooped up from the water and provided welcome extra protein, which had gotten very scarce by this time. At any rate, we knew that as the *putputput* stopped, we had to find cover as fast as we could. Some thirty thousand of the infernal machines were built mostly with slave labor. Ten thousand were fired at and aimed for London, but only one quarter made it. Another 2,500 were used against Antwerp. Some of them may have failed because of the sabotage by the prisoners building them. Others were shot down by British antiaircraft gunners. Some daredevil pilots would, with their plane's wing under the wing of the V-1, tip the bomb over so that it would go down, preferably over the North Sea. More than six thousand Londoners were killed

by the rockets; another seventeen thousand were wounded. The V-1 was never meant as a tactical precision weapon. As a terror weapon for revenge, it unfortunately did a creditable job.

CHAPTER SEVEN

Dolle Dinsdag (Crazy Tuesday)

ON TUESDAY, SEPTEMBER 4, 1944, the Allied troops had advanced well into Belgium. Rumors spread that Breda—on the south side of the Merwede and only some thirty kilometers from Gorkum and rather close to the southern border of Holland—had been liberated. It was based on a newscast from Radio Orange, the Dutch channel of the BBC. It turned out to be false. The Allied troops did indeed reach and conquer the city of Antwerp, in Belgium and not in Holland, although Breda was not that far away across the border. The message was repeated on the next day, September 5.

It had a major impact, both on the Germans and their collaborators and on the Dutch. Both groups felt that the end of the war was near. The Dutch took to the streets, and many were dancing to celebrate. Red, white, and blue flags of the Netherlands and orange flags (the color of the Dutch royal family, the House of Orange, is obviously orange) appeared everywhere. Despite the joint threats—by the Reichskommissar Arthur Seyss-Inquart (six and a quart for the Dutch) and Hans Rauter, the leader of the police, (including the Dutch) and the SS—that there was a state of siege, which warranted the immediate death penalty for any resistance to the Germans or fraternization with the enemy, the Dutch celebrated. An intriguing fact of population statistics is that around nine months after this celebration, significantly more Dutch babies were born than the norm. Two years earlier at the time that the deportations of the Jews began, the opposite happened, and far fewer babies were born. Fear seemed to spread like an infectious disease among the enemy. Many NSBers and other collaborators with the Germans and even German military were packing it in and were lining up at several railway stations to flee to Germany. Apparently, they thought that the end was near. Then the Dutch railways were called on by the Dutch government in exile in London to go on strike again, so the personnel of the trains did not resume work until after the liberation on May 5, 1945. One of the NSBers who fled to Germany was the mayor of Gorinchem, Ir. H. Holtke. When it became clear that the liberation would not happen any time soon, the flags went back in storage and the deserters gradually drifted back. Holtke had a surprise waiting for him after he returned to the city hall of Gorinchem early in October. Dr. Schwebel, representative of the Reichskommissar, told him that he was fired and had two weeks to train a new mayor, E. A. Kolkers.

The progress of the Allied through France and Belgium had completely stagnated because of the speed with which the offensive had progressed, and the army supply lines had been outrun, not being able to keep up. There was only one day's worth of gasoline available for the trucks and tanks, and most of it was reserved for Operation Market Garden. This took place for eight days from September 17 to 25 in 1944. It was a daring and imaginative but risky plan by the British field marshal Bernard Montgomery and approved by the supreme commander, General Dwight Eisenhower. At the end of 1944, around Christmastime, a second major event—the Battle of the Bulge or the Ardennes offensive—took all the Allied power to prevent the breakout attempts of the Germans to retake Antwerp and to cut the Allied forces in two. For the Dutch, it meant that the part of the Netherlands above the Rhine and the other great rivers did not get liberated until May 5, 1945. This postponement led to the winter of 1944–1945 becoming known as the Hunger Winter with some twenty-five thousand Dutch in the western part of the country starving to death.

CHAPTER EIGHT

Operation Market Garden

THE IDEA FOR Market Garden, unquestionably, was brilliant but came with high risk. Any kink in the cable might lead to failure. The basic object was to create a northward one-hundred-kilometer salient into the terrain held by the Germans. Advantages were that it would bypass the major line of defense in West Germany, the Siegfried Line; it would create (via a bridge across the Rhine) direct access to the northern plains of Germany (ideal flat terrain for tank maneuvers) and a straighter approach to Berlin; it would catch the Ruhr area (where the most important German industries were located) in a pincer movement; and it would shorten the war by as much as a year. It was an audacious plan requiring the use of massive airborne operations as well as large numbers of ground troops.

In my town, we did not see any of the operation, except that unusually large numbers of airplanes came flying over in an eastern direction. In 1946, we went camping with a bunch of kids at the Veluwe, in the area where much of the fighting had taken place. There was a fair amount of interesting stuff still lying around, such as spent cartridges, but nothing of much use except a small woodstove, which was promptly pressed into service to make pancakes. I also found a small snake, and I ran off like crazy, thinking that it might come after me.

The basic idea for the operation was relatively simple. Ground troops would go up the main Highway 69 from Eindhoven in the south to Nijmegen and on to Arnhem, about one hundred kilometers up north. There were nine bridges —some wide, some narrow—as part of the route, and paratroopers were to be dropped to secure those. This required close coordination between air and ground forces so that the ground forces would be able to take over from the paratroopers timely enough progress would be unimpeded. The highway was relatively narrow (two lanes, slow going), and the berms were soft enough that outflanking operations were nearly impossible. Nevertheless, the ground troops (XXX Army Corps) were able to move quickly and were able to secure four of the five bridges assigned to them. The bridge over the Wilhelmina Canal at Son had been blown up by German soldiers before it could be taken by the American 101st Airborne Division. This stopped the progress of the XXX Army Corps. However, they were able to close the gap by building a Bailey bridge. This caused a twelve-hour delay, but they made up for it and arrived at the Nijmegen Bridge on time. The plan had been for the American Eighty-Second Airborne Division to have secured the major bridge across the Waal River (which is a major branch of the Rhine on its way to the Rhine Delta). With this goal not accomplished, XXX Army Corps had to conquer the bridge themselves. The result was a thirty-six-hour delay before it was possible for XXX Army Corps to keep on going toward Arnhem, where the British First Airborne Division was barely holding on. Nevertheless, at the end of the first day, the XXX Army Corps, with the associated airborne operations, had been reasonably successful with all bridges or other water crossings in Allied hands except for the bridge in Nijmegen.

On the same day, good progress was being made from the south. The other part at the northern end of the salient of the operations was seriously handicapped because, totally unexpectedly, the Ninth SS Division and the Tenth SS Panzer Division—together forming the II SS Panzer Corps—had been relocated to the area of Nijmegen and Arnhem after heavy fighting in the Falaise Pocket in France. They had lost some 30 percent of their strength and were ordered to rest and refit. This knowledge was actually available to the Allied High Command from three sources: First, the British Code and Cypher School had decoded German radio traffic and produced intelligence reports code named Ultra that were sent to senior army commanders. Second, aerial photographs of the Arnhem area were available from a reconnaissance plane.

And third, information about the presence of the Panzer Corps had been provided by the Dutch resistance. Montgomery dismissed all of it and refused to change the plans for the landing of the British First Airborne Division. A second serious problem was that radio communications between air and ground forces were virtually absent because the equipment simply did not work at all or frequencies of available equipment were not calibrated. Other equipment had an inadequate effective range of only five kilometers. The First British Airborne Division began landing half of its troops around midday at landing zones north and west of Arnhem. One-half of the force was needed to protect the drop zones for the arrival of the second half of the division the next day. Thus, only one quarter of the force was available to advance toward their target, the Arnhem Bridge. The Reconnaissance Squadron was to speed in their jeeps toward the bridge and hold it until the arrival of the brigade; they ran into significant resistance and were unable to proceed. The Second Parachute Battalion advanced eastward toward the Arnhem Bridge on a southern road near the Rhine. The road was nearly undefended, and by evening, they reached the northern end of the bridge. They were joined by the Brigade Headquarters Company. These two units were the only ones that reached the bridge. The next day, the remnants of the First and Third Parachute Battalions of about two hundred men had fought their way into Arnhem, with heavy losses of their officers and noncommissioned officers. Their strength was down to about one-sixth of their normal strength. They were less than two kilometers from the bridge. The Second Lift was delayed due to fog and poor weather but landed in full strength later in the day. At 3:00 a.m. on the third day, a British force of four battalions attacked toward the Arnhem Bridge but ran into heavy resistance from the main German defense line. The paratroopers received heavy casualties, and with no possibility to breakthrough, the five hundred remaining troops withdrew toward Oosterbeek, where the main force was located. The Second Batallion had dug in around the northern access to the bridge and many adjacent houses. German infantry attacks were repulsed, and realizing that this approach was unproductive, the German artillery started shelling the British perimeter using artillery, tanks, and mortars. They systematically pulverized each house, which then allowed the infantry to dislodge the defenders, in which they made slow but steady progress. A two- hour truce was agreed on to remove the many wounded, who became German captives. There was a severe lack of ammo, food, water, and medical supplies. The British paratroopers continued to fight, with knifes if nothing else was available; but by Wednesday morning, the fourth day, most had become prisoners. The last message sent by radio was, "Out of ammo, God save the king." The original plan was for a force of ten thousand to keep the bridge for two days before being released by other troops. It was evidence for the quality of the paratroopers that some 740 men held the northern-bridge approach for four days. The fighting was not done with the loss of the Arnhem Bridge. Fights continued all along Route 69 as the Germans tried to cut off the route of supplies and reinforcements. The Nijmegen Bridge had not been taken by the Eighty-Second Airborne and had to be taken by units from the XXX Army. Four tanks of the Guards Armoured Division crossed the bridge with the German explosive charges not being activated. However, some two hundred German soldiers were in the bridge girders and from there, dropped grenades toward the tanks. They were also attacked with Panzerfausts (bazooka-like weapons). One tank was destroyed; another, damaged, although still moving.

In Oosterbeek, almost 3,600 survivors of the First Airborne Division held on to this bridgehead over the Rhine, intending to hold on till the arrival of XXX Army. On day 5, the remainder of the Independent Polish Brigade was dropped under heavy fire on the south side of the Rhine, losing 25 percent of their strength. On day 9 (September 25, 1944), the First Airborne Division was ordered to withdraw. With the help of British and Canadian engineers, they crossed the Rhine; and by morning, 2,398 survivors had been rescued. Unfortunately, 300 men were left behind and were made prisoners. The First Airborne Division had 10,600 men at the beginning of Market Garden— 1,485 were killed; 6,414 were wounded; and one-third of these were prisoners. The main goal of the operation was not reached as no bridge over the Rhine was taken and held. This was the largest airborne operation of the Second World War and perhaps ever, with 34,600 paratroopers (with 20,000 landed by parachutes, the rest by glider).

CHAPTER NINE

Battle of the Bulge

AFTER THE ALLIED forces broke out from Normandy about six weeks after the invasion of D-Day, they moved quicker than anticipated toward Germany. The troops were tired after many weeks of continued combat. Supplies were dangerously low, and the supply lines were stretched. An organization of a large number of trucks named the Red Ball Express transported supplies to the front line, but this was prohibitively costly. It took five gallons of gasoline to get one gallon to the front. By early October, the Allies suspended any major military offenses to improve their supply lines and build up supplies at the front. The Ardennes—a densely wooded terrain of high hills and deep valleys, with a relatively sparse road network—did not seem to need more than limited troops for its defense. Adolf Hitler came up with the idea of a counteroffensive through the Ardennes, the goals being to split the Allied forces, exploiting the partially imagined and partially real discord between the American and the British forces, and to regain Antwerp with its harbor. Once the separation of the Allied had occurred and Antwerp had been captured, four complete Allied armies would be caught without supplies or means to obtain them behind German lines. Hitler could then compel the Allies to negotiate a peace treaty. This would allow the German troops of the western front to be transferred to the eastern front, where the Russian armies had made rapid progress. Both Generalfeldmarschalls Walter Model (Army Group BD) and Gerd von Runstedt (commander-in-chief armies in the West) felt that Hitler's plans were too ambitious and unlikely to succeed. But Hitler persisted.

Preparation for the operation took place in total secret. Major contributions to this success were the poor weather, which did not allow Allied reconnaissance flights, and the excellent telephone system in Germany, in which the radio traffic was not needed. Thus, the Enigma machine providing the Ultra intelligence was not able to measure any messages. Minor potential problems were not neglected. For instance, cooks were provided with charcoal rather than wood for the kitchen fires to reduce smoke. Yet there were two intelligence officers, Col. Oscar Koch from First Army and BG Kenneth Strong from SHAEF, who suspected the attack; but their information was not taken into consideration.

The northern arm of the planned offensive was given top priority for supplies and the shortest distance to Antwerp. After Hitler was almost killed the previous July 20 in an assassination attempt in which several Wehrmacht officers played a role, he lost trust in the army and preferred the SS. The Sixth Panzer Army under command of SS Oberstgruppenfuhrer Sepp Dietrich had several SS divisions, including two SS Panzer Divisions. The middle sector had the Fifth Panzer Army with the objective Brussels, and the Seventh Army had the southern sector and had the task to protect the southern flank. One special group of English-speaking German soldiers— Operation Greif, under command of Col. Otto Skorzeny—was to sow confusion behind the Allied lines. They were dressed in American or British uniforms with the appropriate dog tags. They had to reroute traffic, destroy signposts, and seize bridges across the Meuse River. This had no major influence on the outcome of the overall battle although they definitely sowed confusion. When caught, they were considered spies and were executed. The entire task force was readied in total secret, which was aided by poor weather, preventing aerial reconnaissance.

On December 16, at 5:30 a.m., the Allies were totally surprised by a massive artillery bombardment by 1,600 artillery pieces over a 130-kilometer front. In the northern sector, the attack was led by a *Kampfgruppe* commanded by Stormbannfuhrer Joachim Peiper. The route chosen toward Elsenborn Ridge (essential for providing coverage) was blocked by collapsed overpasses. They were rerouted to the village of Lanzerath. This was to be taken by five hundred infantrymen from the Third Regiment Fallschirmjaeger, but eighteen men from a reconnaissance platoon from the Ninety-Ninth Division Infantry were able to hold the Germans up until four in the afternoon, causing almost one hundred German casualties. The Peiper group was delayed by over sixteen hours. Next day, they encountered only lightly armed elements of the 285th Artillery Observation Battalion. After a brief fight, they surrendered and were sent to stand in a field. When the main body of the Peiper group arrived, the SS suddenly opened fire on the American prisoners. A few escaped, but eighty-four were murdered. Driving southeast, they encountered a Ninety-Ninth Division rest center, filled with confused American soldiers. Several dozen were made prisoners and were also murdered. Another incident occurred close to Saint Vith where eleven black American soldiers surrendered, were tortured, and then shot. On the other side, American soldiers shot some sixty German prisoners of war near the village of Chenogne on New Year's Day in 1945.

Fighting continued, but progress for the units of the Sixth Panzer Army was slow and was eventually stopped due to the stiff resistance of the Ninety- Ninth Infantry Division, even though they were outnumbered five to one. They inflicted casualties to the Germans in a ratio of eighteen to one. They lost 465 who were killed, but the German losses were much higher at more than 4,000 killed. The ultimate goal—the bridges over the Meuse (or Maas) River, essential for the further progress toward Antwerp—was never reached.

In the center sector, the 5th Panzer Army was opposed to the thinly spread

28th and 106th divisions; two American regiments were surrounded in a pincer move and had to surrender. Some eight thousand men and their equipment were lost, the most serious setback suffered by the American forces in the 1944–45 campaigns in the European theater. The village of Saint Vith was held by the Americans until Field Marshall Montgomery ordered their withdrawal. The German plans had called for Saint Vith, a vital road junction, to be in their hands by December 17; and because they were not successful until December 23, this was a major setback. The Ninth Panzer Division made rapid headway toward the bridges in Dinant but over a rather narrow corridor. When this was threatened, they halted their advance; their access to the bridges in and around Dinant was blocked by a mixture of rear echelon troops, MPs and army air force personnel.

In the southern sector, two German columns were moving westward: one was north; and one, south of Bastogne. Both had been engaged several times and slowed down considerably. But on December 21, they had advanced enough to surround Bastogne. The town was defended by the 101st Airborne Division with additional strength by the all African American 969th Artillery

Battalion and the Combat Command B of the 10th Armored Division. Conditions for the American troop were difficult. Medical supplies and most of the medical personnel were captured, food supplies were almost exhausted, and artillery ammunition was running out. Fortunately, four of the next five days, the weather cleared. Supplies could be dropped, and the

American troops held their perimeter. The German commander, Generalleutnant von Lüttwitz, asked for the surrender of Bastogne; and the commander of the 101st Division, Brigadier General McAuliffe, wrote back "Nuts," a response that has become famous. Two German Panzer Divisions moved forward from Bastogne to attack the main American line but were defeated; their tanks were destroyed. The day after Christmas, the Fourth Armored Division and the Twenty-Sixth Infantry Division, under the command of General Patton, broke through and opened a corridor to Bastogne.

By December 24, the German attacks in all three sectors were stalled and none of the bridges over the Meuse were in German hands. General von Manteuffel proposed to Hitler that all offensive actions be stopped and that the troops be withdrawn back to Germany. Hitler did not approve of this. A counterattack, primarily by the German Luftwaffe (air force), led to the destruction or damaging of almost five hundred Allied planes. However, losses by the Luftwaffe were so large that it was ineffective for the remainder of the war. By January 7, 1945, Hitler agreed that all the German forces were to withdraw from the Ardennes, and they executed a mostly successful fighting withdrawal. But most of their tanks stayed behind and were lost due to an almost total lack of fuel. Fighting continued until January 25 when the last German units made it back to their starting point. Numbers vary depending on their source. German strength at its highest consisted of 450,000 troops. Casualties were up to 98,000. American troops at their peak numbered 610,000 and suffered 89,000 casualties. This includes killed, missing, wounded, and captured. The character and size of these two events, Operation Market Garden and the Battle of the Bulge, were epic; but it took another five months to end the war in Europe.

CHAPTER TEN

Second Evacuation

IN NOVEMBER 1944, the German authorities declared that all homes in neighborhoods on the south side of Gorinchem had to be cleared out with as little as two days' notice. The vacated houses were to be locked, and the keys were to be handed over to the police at city hall. It was up to the inhabitants of the house to find another place to stay. If they could not find anything, city hall might be able to offer some assistance. The reason for vacating the homes close to the river probably was due to the expectation of the occupying forces that Allied troops might try to cross the Merwede River. Dad found a place with the family Zijl in the Arkelstraat. Mr. Zijl was old, probably in his seventies or even eighties. He was a retired army sergeant major. We never saw him, and he lived with his daughter Marie on the second floor. Marie was around sixty, and we did think that she was not very nice, a typical spinster. We went from living in a four-story large house to being in a suite of two rooms on the first floor, and our mother could use the kitchen at lunchtime. There was a toilet, but I do not remember a bathroom. And I believe that we were washed by Mom and her sister Tante Leen, standing in a tub of water that had been heated on the stove. The only soap still available was "green soap," a paste-like green mass normally used for laundry, cleaning the floors, and the like. A bath was no fun. The room was cold, and the hot water quickly cooled off. My aunt, who often washed us, was a nurse; and she used a pretty hard brush on us to be sure we were clean. We ended up with nicely pink or red skin. My grandfather and Aunt Helen were forced to abandon their home in Den Helder, near the sea in the northern part of the province in North Holland. The Germans had vacated and then demolished all the houses near the North Sea, anticipating a possible Allied landing, which never came, at least not in this area. Thus, we had a full house—my little sister, Irene, who was about one year old; us four brothers; my parents; grandfather; and aunt, for a total of nine people, quite a lot for our limited space. Irene would sit in her child's chair in front of one of the two tall windows looking out on the street, where there was always something to see. My mom had just taken her out of the chair to feed her when suddenly there was a very loud noise, and pieces of glass were flying everywhere. There was a horse's head looking through the splintered window. Apparently, two Ukranians on a horse and wagon—probably loaded with stolen sugar beets—lost control of their horse. They came down the Walsteeg way too fast, did not make the turn into the Arkelstraat, and ended up in our room. Thanks to a mother's intuition, Irene had been taken out of her chair just in the neck of time. Or maybe thanks to a lot of luck; Irene ended up without a scratch. Window glass was not available for any money because of all the broken glass from the bomb attacks, so the open window was repaired with wooden boards. The very same thing happened once more, with the horse and wagon coming through the wood closing the window.

Early in the new year, our dad was arrested. He went to the house of a "patient," not for medical reasons but to warn him about German plans for a raid to catch several members of the resistance. How dad had obtained this information, I do not know. It is possible that there was some Dutch worker in the German headquarters who acted as a spy. When he came to the house, the "patient" was not there. He had been arrested, but two members of the *Landwacht* (country guard) were hidden there, intent to catch any visitor to the house. The Landwacht was the result of an agreement between Ir. Mussert, the leader of the NSB (the political party in favor of the Germans) and Rauter, the head of police and SS in the country. They organized the Netherland's Landwacht, a nationwide corps, which essentially became an extension of the police forces in the country and particularly worked with the German Gestapo. Professional Landwachters worked full-time and on salary; others were part-time and got paid by the hour. The advantage for the Germans was that the Landwacht was drawn from the local population and therefore, usually was well-informed about local conditions. Dad was arrested by the Landwachters and brought to our house. He was searched there under the curious eyes of some of his children. His vaccination equipment was discovered, and the metal cylinder that held a syringe and needles was immediately declared to be a bomb. They told dad to go outside in the garden and demonstrate opening the cylinder while the Landwachters took cover behind a low stone wall. After being convinced that there would be no explosion, they took dad to the headquarters of the Gestapo. He stuck to his story that he was just trying to check on one of his patients; and fortunately, he was released after two or three days, to the relief and delight of his wife and kids.

CHAPTER ELEVEN

Heat and Light

IT WAS A cold fall and an even colder winter in 1944–45. Most of the time, no electricity was available unless you were lucky enough to have a German officer or soldier quartered in your house. Then you had electricity, at least, in the part of the house where the German was located. However, the civilians living in the same house were not supposed to turn it on. You could be punished pretty severely if caught. Also, when it was dark, not a single ray of light was allowed to escape and become visible. We did have some nightly bombardments by Allied planes, but I don't know if those were invited by visible light. I heard that soldiers would even shoot through your windows if they saw light. People became quite inventive in improvising a light source. Candles would have been an ideal solution, but those were tough to get. If you had paraffin or something similar, you could make your own. I remember doing my homework by the light of a *drijvertje* or a floater. This was made with a small triangle of flat tin, perhaps obtained from an old can, some three centimeters big. A small hole was made in the center for a wick, a piece of rope or an old shoelace. Tiny pieces of cork were stuck on the three corners to make it float on the surface of a glass jar with some oil in it. It did not give a lot of light, but it was enough to read by. Some handymen would set up a stationary bike with a dynamo on the moving wheel, and as long as somebody peddled the bike, they had some light. Staying warm and cooking were even more of a problem. The gas factory was closed because most of the coal was gone. Most people had been dependent on gas or coal for their warmth and for their kitchen stove. We had a small *nood kachel* (emergency stove) made by the local steel fabric De

Vries Robbé and had to have wood of trees and branches to keep the stove going. Mom may have had limited access to the furnace of the landlady as well. People were desperate, and some hacked their furniture or parts of their homes to pieces to get firewood. We did not have to resort to that. One day, my younger brothers Jan and Kees came home with an entire midsized tree, which was growing on the city wall, and they had chopped it down. They schlepped it through the corridor in the middle of the house into the garden, where it was disassembled into firewood. Marie was not too happy with all the twigs and leaves broken off during the transport toward the garden and insisted that we clean up the corridor right away. Another much more dangerous source for wood were the trenches that the occupiers had dug or that they had forced to be dug by forced laborers, in the top of the city walls. Their sides had been re-enforced with wooden boards. You could break the boards loose and have another source of firewood, but you better not be caught at it. The stove was not very large, but it had a broad flattop, which could hold several pots and pans on the top. That way, the heat going to the chimney with the smoke was available once again before going up the chimney. There was no school at this time for several reasons. There was no coal to burn the stoves needed to heat the classrooms, and many teachers had gone underground. So my parents and their friends organized a small class in the office of a car dealer for at least a few hours per day. I got lessons from a retired teacher in the afternoon for about two hours. Of course, when you are the sole person getting all that attention from your teacher, you can move pretty quickly, certainly at elementary school level. And by the time school started again, I was a full year ahead of the class and could skip a year. One day, four of my friends were waiting for me at the end of the lesson, one of them on stilts. A discussion developed about the possibility of tipping a hat from somebody's head with a stilt, and pretty soon, it developed into a dare. A man walked by wearing a hat; so I took the stilt, sneaked behind him, and took a swing at the hat. I missed and hit him square in the back of his head. He turned and came after me like a raging bull. I dropped the stilt and ran faster than I ever had run before. Around the corner, I flew into the back garden of Mrs.

Kassander, a patient of my dad. The man still came after me, so I ran into her house and hid behind the couch. When he came in, he was confronted by Mrs. Kassander, asking him what he was doing in her house and telling him to leave. When the coast was clear, I went home, where my parents already knew what had happened. To make things worse, the man was a deacon in our church. Dad told me to go offer my apologies, and with lead in my shoes, I went to the man's house and rang the bell. The door opened to tall stairs going to a second-floor home. There was no way I was going up there. When someone appeared at the top of the stairs, I yelled as loud as I could, "I am here to offer my apologies. I am sorry!" And with that, I was gone.

Unbeknownst to me, Mrs. Kassander was also a member of the Resistance as a courier. She bicycled to farms in the environment of Gorkum to deliver messages about possible German raids so that the Dutch partisans, the hiding Jews, and Allied pilots and other fliers could hide. Often I rode with her on the bike's passenger seat, not knowing what the real purpose of the trip was. Perhaps I was a decoy as the German soldiers liked kids. Her adult son used to collect postage stamps and proposed to trade it to me for some tobacco. Of course, I did not have any, but dad gave me a small amount from his rapidly dwindling supply (what a sacrifice!). So I had my stamp album.

CHAPTER TWELVE

Hunger

DURING 1944, FOOD supplies became increasingly scarce, particularly in the western part of the country above the Great Rivers. This was where the large cities were located—Amsterdam, Rotterdam, and The Hague. There were several reasons why food supplies were so low. When the Dutch government in exile in London asked the Dutch railway to go on strike, the German administration in retaliation placed an embargo on all food transports to the western part of Holland. This made the food problem much worse. By the time the embargo was partially lifted in November, most of the waterways were frozen solidly, and transport by ship had become impossible. The Allied pilots could not differentiate between German ships with a military purpose and the food transports. The people in the big cities survived by eating sugar beets and tulip and other flower bulbs and whatever they could find, such as cats, dogs, and rats. As an example of how bad it was, the bread ration for a week was 2,200 grams in the early fall. By October, it was 1,000 grams; and by April 1945, it had been reduced to 400 grams. The people in Rotterdam and other cities were starving, and although the reported numbers vary, some twenty-five thousand starved to death. In Gorkum, things were not nearly as bleak since it was located in the middle of a large agricultural region. While some farmers and black marketeers abused the situation and increased their prices for grain and so on sky-high, others were more reasonable. For instance, my dad was able to obtain a large burlap sack filled with wheat grain. I believe he traded it for the typewriter from his practice. He also finagled a supply of rapeseed oil. Our other source of fat was suet. My mother was a master in cooking up something from minimal supplies. She baked all our bread from the wheat, using some yeast coming from the baker. Often it was my job or my brothers' to grind the wheat grain in an old coffee mill into flour. I vividly remember the smell of the bread being baked and its taste. Maybe that is why I like to bake my own bread.

Mom would put some rapeseed oil or melted suet on the slice of bread instead of butter, which did not exist anymore. Then instead of jam or cheese, she would put on a layer of finely cut carrots or onions. Sometimes she used thin slices of apple. On rare occasions, there was syrup made from sugar beets or the leftover cracklings left over from the melting of the suet. They were little pieces of connective tissue, little blood vessels, and so on that got fried. One day, I was in the kitchen and saw a pan on the furnace with mashed potatoes mixed with some vegetable. I was hungry and took a small spoonful from the pan and put it in my mouth. Suddenly somebody grabbed me by my hair, roughly turned me around, and hit me in the face. It was Marie! She yelled at me, "You are a thief! You will grow up for the gallows and the wheel. Don't let me catch you again." I never stepped in the kitchen again unless my mother was there.

Another source of food came from the central kitchen. This began in 1943 when some of the Dutchmen found it difficult to get enough food. But in the fall and winter of 1944/45, use of the central kitchen became necessary for most people. The city leaders foresaw that the coming winter would get rough for everybody. They had actually hired a large parcel of land on the south side of the river, and the owner had agreed to grow mostly potatoes and cabbage. But when harvest time came, he refused to go near the area because it was too dangerous with bullets and other deadly projectiles flying around. Some volunteers went across the river to harvest the food so that the central kitchen got its supplies. The product was not exactly gourmet food. One of us, often me, had to go to one of the places of distribution and bring a pail or a pot. Our family's portion was put in the pail. It was usually a thin stew or soup from potatoes and cabbage. It was not the greatest, but it was food. One time, I found the lower jaw of a pig in the pot; another time, part of a brush. My sister, Irene, was just a year old; and she needed milk. There was a dairy farm just outside the Arkel gate and not far from our evacuation home, and an arrangement had been made with the farmer that we would get one quart of milk every day. It became my job to pick it up, so I would go to the farm with a pan to get it. This was a real treasure. Regular milk and its products, butter and cheese, had not been available for a while. One time, in the middle of the winter, I saw a dead calf lying in the snow outside the stable. It was quite small, maybe prematurely born. I was thinking what a waste this was and thought about asking the farmer if I could take it home to clean it up and skin it and then eat it, but I did not dare. German officers were quartered next door, which was a hotel. Army cars and trucks were parked there; and in one of those, the Germans had made an improvised chicken coop, which meant they had eggs. Jan and Kees had more guts than I did. I was not such a hero, and at times, they would sneak into the chicken coop and steal the eggs. It was a risky business; at the least, they would have gotten a good beating or worse if they had been caught. Luckily, that never happened. The eggs were not the only thing that we stole. After all, stealing from the enemy was a good thing. Sugar also had disappeared long ago. Every day, large wagons loaded to the brim with sugar beets, confiscated from the farms, passed through our street. That was quite a temptation. We would sneak behind the wagon and grab some of the beets. The lower ones were the easiest to get but when pulled out, sometimes would cause a little avalanche of the ones located higher up. The Ukranians seated in front and directing the pulling of horses usually would not bother to look, and the high stacks of beets were in the way. The beets were cut into small pieces and then boiled in water. When they were soft, they were mashed and put through a sieve. The juice would stand on our *nood kachel* for hours to evaporate most of the water, and the end result was a thick syrup. The room had a nauseating smell while this was going on, but the result was worth it, something sweet to put on bread and in the ersatz coffee. I am not sure how the pseudo coffee was made. Sometimes essence (imitation) of orange or vanilla was added to the syrup for special occasions. *Kuch*, sourdough bread, for the German troops was baked in a building in the Keizerstraat, the Gas-School. One guy would cart it on a wagon to the *kazerne* where the troops were quartered. On the way, the soldier would always stop off at a café to fortify himself. The cart stood outside with no guard, and that was the time to steal some *kuch*. However, if he saw you, he would shoot.

In March 1945, an agreement was reached between the Germans and the Allies: the Germans would not shoot at the airplanes coming over, and the Allies would not bomb their installations. This made it possible for the Royal Air Force, for the Royal Canadian Air Force, and for the US Army Air Force to fly mercy flights, delivering flour donated by the Swedish and the Swiss Red Cross. The flour was baked into breads in Holland, but it became known as Swedish bread. Its distribution began to solve the hunger crisis in the west of Holland. I remember very well going with a tote bag to a distribution point on the Hoogstraat. While I walked home with white breads and a package of margarine, I could not resist, so I wormed a little hole in the paper around the margarine and tasted a little morsel with my pinkie. I also broke a minimal piece of crust from the bread. It was the best taste I had in a long time. Some interesting medical facts came out of the hunger winter. I was taught in medical school that there was less diabetes mellitus and hypertension. Perhaps more interesting is the finding that children with coeliac disease did better on their hunger diet. When bread became available again, the disease returned almost immediately. The pediatrician Dr. Willem Dicke was able to prove that the gluten in wheat was the culprit. Not only did people go hungry but food for cows and pigs was scarce as well. The peelings of potatoes and, to a lesser extent, other vegetables were placed in a basket and placed outside for collection to be used as animal food. Sometimes people would leave a peeling knife, which sometimes was swallowed by the animal; and then the cow/pig would have something "sharp in", which was potentially deadly.

It was clear that the war and the German occupation were coming to an end, but the Germans still initiated a number of destructive actions presumably for defense against the Allied military. They opened the lock doors to inundate large tracts of land. They blew up a number of tall buildings, such as water towers and windmills, that might be used as observation posts. They were even considering to demolish the Great Tower in Gorinchem dating back to the fifteenth century. Fortunately, plans changed, and the tower was safe. There may have been some military justification for these measures; but others, such as the destruction of the infrastructure in the harbor of Rotterdam, just seemed vengeful. Some new terror announcements were made. One seemed really bizarre: scrubbing of the street carried the death penalty.

CHAPTER THIRTEEN

Liberation

ON MAY 4, 1945, it was announced that the capitulation of the German forces in the Netherlands, Denmark, and Northwest Germany would become effective the next morning, May 5 at 8:00 a.m. After five years minus five days, the war was over, at least, in Western Europe; and we were free. The war in the Netherlands East Indies (now Indonesia) against Japan would go on for another four months. That meant that the worrying was not over for many Dutch families who had relatives in the East Indies. Three uncles, who were brothers of my dad, with their wives and kids lived there. But now it was time for celebration.

Dutch (red, white, and blue) flags were everywhere, as were the orange ones, symbolic of the ties to the royal family. The streets were full of people wearing orange clothing of some kind—sweaters, shawls, shirts, or whatever. There were parades with marching bands in front and many dancing and singing people behind. The German troops were still around, and the celebrating men and women were strongly counseled not to provoke or otherwise insult the German occupiers in order to avoid conflicts and even shootings. When the celebrations became too rambunctious, some shots were in fact fired by German troops but, fortunately, only in the air. At this time, no Allied troops had arrived yet in Gorinchem. The Dutch resistance was no longer underground, and it became the Dutch Binnenlandse Strijdkrachten (Dutch interior forces), the BS. It became visible with Prince Bernhard appointed as the commander in chief. Their uniforms were improvised—blue overalls with armbands, some insignia, and a beret. The resistance was a small organization, but suddenly it became much bigger because more than one individual joined the organization at the last minute, now that there was no longer any danger associated with being a member.

Fig. 13-1: Dad on his motorcycle passing a column of surrendering German troops

In the evening of May 7, the first Allies arrived in a jeep; one of them was a previous Gorkumer. The next morning, a Canadian general, with his staff, arrived at city hall. The night curfew was lifted. In the meantime, the old mayor and the commissioner of the police had been reinstated. Both had been in function before the war had started; and once Holland was occupied, they were replaced by NSB members, collaborators with the Germans. The surrendering German troops deposited their weaponry in the Wilhelmina Park, outside the Watergate, near the river. The park was crisscrossed with trenches meant for the defense against Allied forces if they crossed the river, which never happened. The German soldiers were marched off to collection points; and from there, presumably to Germany. The BS began arresting the collaborators of the Germans, the NSB members, and black marketeers, as well as the women who had entertained friendships with the Germans.

The latter group was transported to the military *kazerne*, and they ended up having their head hair cut off. The people standing around viewed this with great enthusiasm and with a lot of whooping and hollering, but most of Gorkum's citizens did not approve at all of this action. It seemed to be a very childish form of revenge. One of the victims was the daughter of the owner of the next-door hotel, where German officers had been quartered, and she had always been very nice to us.

We were free to return to our own house, and Dad and I went together to check what had happened to it. The house key still worked. Inside it was a holy mess. All the walls had holes in them; apparently, the soldiers quartered in the house (Ukrainians) had been looking for valuables. There was a large hole on the floor of the living room going straight down into my dad's office. There were pools of blood on the floor of the practice and in the garden as well as cow bones—some were large—a rib cage, jawbone, and so on. Apparently, the practice space had been used as a slaughterhouse. In addition to the mess everywhere, there were weapons lying around, including "potato mashers" (German hand grenades) and Panzerfausts (an anti-tank weapon). My dad would not let me take any of the weapons. Against one wall in the garden was a large stack of crates filled with sticks of dynamite. They appeared wet and must have been rained on. We tried to burn them, and they produced just a small oily flame. Human feces were lying outside close to the wall below most windows. It appeared that the Ukrainian soldiers in the house did not use the three toilets in the house but just pooped out of the windows. Obviously, it took more than a month of cleaning and repairs before we could move back in the house.

A lot more food now became available, probably from army supplies. Canned corned beef, small sausages in a tin can, Spam, condensed milk, biscuits of one kind or another, and later dried bananas made us feel we were in a food paradise. Food by itself, however, was not turning war off. Some effects lingered from bombardments—even if you were not afraid during, or not aware of it—with bombs exploding maybe a hundred yards from the house. A bombed out three floors high store on the Hoogstraat, a favorite shopping area, became a favorite play area for kids, despite warning signs forbidding entry.

Removal of the ruins after the end of the war kept on being postponed and a kid got killed by a large piece of the roof falling down. It must have had some influence because for a while, I had recurrences of a dream, in which I was sunning on my back in the grass of a pasture. A silver dot would appear in the blue sky, get closer, and turn into a plane, releasing a bomb that would get bigger and bigger and coming right at me, and I would wake up just before it would hit me. In a variation, a German soldier would throw a hand grenade at me. I also developed some strange eating habits—drinking salad dressing straight from the bottle or stuffing ten cookies in my mouth, one after another. Fortunately, all that disappeared in a few months.

I have asked my siblings about this, and we all agree that we don't remember having had any lasting fear. Sure, there was panic when the air- raid alarms started up or when a V-1 came *put-put-putting* over. But once we were home, we were safe, and it became an adventure.

School did not reopen until September, four months later. My brothers and I were free for all that time and basically were running free to commit all kinds of mischief.

Juvenile Delinquents

I am convinced that if we had done now the stuff we did fifty years ago, we would have been declared juvenile delinquents. The presence of all that war equipment and ammunition with only one Canadian soldier as a guard was irresistible for us kids. We just had to find a way past the guard, and it turned out to be pretty simple.

The Wilhelmina Park was a triangular area outside of the city walls with one point of the triangle directed at the Waterpoort. This was the place where the guard was stationed. When you came out of the poort, the river was on your left; the park was, more or less, in the middle; and the city wall was on the right. You could avoid the guard by climbing down the quay in the water as soon as you came out of the gate. The water here was only a bit more than ankle-deep, and you could wade through it. Once the guard had been passed, it was easy to climb back up out of the water and enter the park to grab some of the goodies, such as cartridges, hand grenades, and packages of powder used to load artillery shells.

There was a large walk-in cabinet in the bedroom of my brother Kees and me. We decided this was a perfect place to hide our hoard and maybe make a small war museum. But we also wanted to try to do something with the stuff. We quickly found out that we did not need firecrackers anymore. We would make a fire and throw a handful of cartridges in it. As soon as they would get hot enough, the cartridges would start to explode, and the bullets would fly around everywhere. So before doing this, we always first looked to find a safe place where we could hide, such as a wall. Hand grenades were a lot more dangerous than bullets, but we only used them in the water. If a grenade explodes underwater, it changes the pressure in the air bladder, and fishes come floating to the surface. All we had to do was scoop them up.

The doorbell rang just as we were getting ready for dinner. Mom asked me to go see who it was. In front of the door stood a Canadian soldier, who was supporting a kid of about my age. He was holding his left arm and hand with his right hand. The hand was really bleeding. Two fingers were missing, and the thumb was hanging on one thread of tissue. He had tried to take the detonator out of a grenade, and it exploded in his hand. My dad took them to the hospital to take care of it. After the excitement died down and dinner was finished, we went to bed. The next morning, we saw that our entire war museum was gone. We could not find it anywhere. At this time, grandfather De Kok, our *opa*, lived with us. He thought that all this military gear was very dangerous, and he took it upon himself to remove the danger by throwing everything in the river.

With no more bullets to play with, we turned to our other favorite playground, the river. Dad had given us a small rowboat. We also had two aluminum canoes. The Allied fighter planes carried an extra fuel tank. After it was emptied, the tank was jettisoned. Their shape reminded me of about six feet of a giant stogie cigar. They made great canoes after we cut a square of aluminum out of one side to make room for sitting down. But they were also very labile, so rollovers were common. We used the canoes on the small Linge River going through the city. To go on the large Merwede River, we could not use the canoes, but we had the rowboat.

The Merwede is a wide, fast-flowing river, one of the main branches of the Rhine, on its way to the North Sea. Its width varies with the time of year. In the early months of the year, when the snow is melting in Switzerland and Germany, it is as wide as five hundred meters.

It was busy day and night with shipping to and from the sea harbor of Rotterdam all the way to Basel, Switzerland, and many places in between. The water was dirty with an oil slick on the surface, which killed off many fish species, such as salmon. The last salmon was caught around 1930. In recent decades, intensive efforts have cleaned up the river a great deal; but at the time I lived in Gorinchem, pollution was bad. It did not stop us from swimming and boating though. The current was so strong that, with our small boat, we could only float downstream, but there were ways to go in the opposite direction. The countercurrent close to the edges was one way to get upstream. The other way was more fun. We rowed the boat toward the side of a fast-running freighter until we were close enough to grab the side, along which, we would let our boat slide toward the back, where we would tie a rope and let our boat be pulled upstream. The skippers did not like what we did. It was dangerous; we could be sucked under the keel and even into the propeller. Once we were attached, we'd go upstream for several miles, loosen the rope, and float downstream. Sometimes we'd go across the river to the southern side and camp there. Our parents were easygoing in that regard, and they trusted that we were not up to any mischief. That trust was sometimes misplaced. One day, an irate shopkeeper came to the door to complain that two of "the boys of the doctor" had been in his store an hour earlier, and now he missed several candy bars. Dad said, "Let's check it out." He called us. "Boys, come here." He put us in a row in the front hall and asked each of us if we were responsible. Everyone denied it. He turned around to the shopkeeper and said, "See, they did not do it." Implicitly, he and Mom always believed us. If the neighbors would call to warn my mother that we were again in our boat on the river doing dangerous things, Mom would thank them for calling and continue her business.

Our rowboat was tied up in the harbor in front of our house. With the winter coming, we decided to take it out of the water and place it on dry ground in our garden, but when we went to get it, it was gone. It might have been stolen by the crew of a ship passing through or maybe it was rammed and sunk. Our adventures on the great river came to an end. But we still challenged one another to swim across, at least in the summer. We still had the canoes made from the gas tanks of the fighter planes. We could take them on the Linge River, go fishing, or find duck eggs.

My Lab

There was an unused small bedroom in the attic, and I thought it would make a perfect lab. There was no way to lock it, so I had to think of some way to keep my younger brothers out if I were to keep chemicals there. At the time, a construction company had been contracted to install new scales behind the city hall close to the Great Church. When they dug a deep hole to place the scales in, they encountered a large number of human bones. Apparently, there had been a church cemetery there, maybe centuries ago. The work had to be stopped until the bones had been gathered for reburial. After working hours, one guy stayed as a guard. When I was talking to him, he told me he was getting a cup of coffee, and he walked away. I hopped over the fence and hurried into the hole and found an intact skull, brown from its years underground; and I took it home, up to my lab. I mounted it on a small shelf across from the door and put small red lights in the eye sockets. I drilled a small hole in the doorframe and fixed an old copper clad rod there and put a small metal plate on top of the door. When the door opened, the two touched and closed a circuit so that the red lights came on; they flickered because the rod was flexible and was moved. It worked very well. My younger brothers and sister and even the maids stayed away! I found an old book used by dad for the course he gave in civil defense in the years before the war.

The first experiment was to make chlorine gas by mixing hydrochloric acid and a cleaning substance in a flask. I did not see much other than some green color, so I shook the flask and smelled.

I thought I was going to die. Luckily, I had taken a very shallow breath; otherwise, I was sure I would have kicked the bucket. After all, chlorine gas killed tens of thousands of soldiers during the First World War. Although my enthusiasm was cooled somewhat, I did still try to make an explosive. It did not explode, but it burst into flames. I lost some of my eyebrows, and the front of my scalp hair was a bit shortened. I found a recipe in dad's old book to make a gas that smelled like rotten eggs, "stink bombs." It turned out to be simple. I mixed the ingredients together, and within a few minutes, it really stank. It seemed a good thing to try out at the weekly catechism course at our church, a rather boring hour of learning old rules in archaic language. I was a bit early in the class, and I hid the "bomb" under a cabinet. The minister came in and started the lesson. Then he kind of stuck his nose in the air and sniffed. He closed the door and the windows and started his lecture as if all was normal. After he was done, he turned around and asked who made this awful smell. I stuck up my hand, and he sent everybody else home. I thought that I was in real trouble, thinking that he would say.

"Now you have done it," .However, he said that this time, he would not punish me because I had been honest about it but I better not do it again. I went home with a hell of a headache, so I did a little more reading and found that the gas was actually poisonous. I felt that this was a good time to abandon the explosive and other experiments and maybe pick up another hobby, like setting up a herbarium.

Mom's Birthday

My mom's birthday was January 1, and we wanted to get her a present. But not much was available as yet, plus we had no money. So we decided to make something for her. She was always sewing and repairing things, and a needle holder seemed a good present. With a sawed-off piece of a branch, we went to the subbasement, where the heart of the central heating was located. We opened the door and held a poker into the glowing cokes until it was red-hot. We then stuck it in the branch to gradually burn it out and to create a hollow tube. It took quite a number of returning the poker to the hot coal, so the subbasement was full of smoke. With the tube, we went off to the bedroom/playroom of my younger brothers, planning to burn some decorations with a hot needle on the tube's surface. We found an old cookie jar and filled it up with kerosene. An old shoelace made a perfect wick. It was lighted, and we heated a needle in the flame, planning to start burning a pattern. Unfortunately, at that time, the shoelace fell into the cookie jar; so all the kerosene began to burn, producing clouds of black smoke and soot. I grabbed the burning cookie jar, opened a window, and threw the jar out the window on the street. We opened the remaining windows and tried, not very successfully, to get the smoke out of the room. Mom was in the kitchen, and she had a nose like a bloodhound's. Pretty soon, she came running up the stairs and started banging on the door. "What the heck is going on? Open the door right now." My brother Pim had hidden in the cabinet, and Jan climbed between the wall and the Murphy bed. I was the oldest, and it was left up to me to open the door. And when Mom saw the smoke and then discovered that the jar had burned a nice black square in the carpet belonging to her sister, she gave me some hits on my head with her shoe (she had a vascular tumor on the mouse of her hand and could not hit with it). They did not really hurt, but I felt insulted. After all, the problems had arisen while we were trying to make her birthday present. I decided to run away and walked around in the city; but after two hours, I started to feel hungry and thought, *I better return home.*

Vacation

In the summer of 1946, we went for the first time on a family vacation. My parents had rented a farmhouse on Tessel (or Texel) while the farm family lived in their barn for the summer. Tessel is an island in the North Sea, north of Den Helder, an easy ferry ride away.

In 1945, an infantry battalion of the German army was quartered on the island. It consisted of some four hundred Germans and eight hundred Georgians as part of the defense along the European coast against an Allied invasion. The Georgians had been recruited the same way as the Ukrainians were elsewhere. They had been made prisoners of war, and they were kept under very miserable conditions. When given the chance to enlist in the German army, many did. But the Georgians never liked the Germans, and this became worse after the Allied forces had landed and were fighting their way through Europe. They began talking about revolting against the Germans and trying to link up with the Allied. The plans became concrete action on the night of April 5–6, 1945. The Georgians killed their German comrades. A few Germans escaped to Den Helder and sounded the alarm. More German troops were ferried to Tessel until there were about three thousand on the island. Brutal fighting followed, where no quarter was given or asked by either side. In some instances, Dutch citizens had fought with the Georgians, and many others had been hiding them and providing them with food and other necessities even though the Germans announced that anyone caught giving assistance in any form to the Georgians would be executed and would have their houses or farms burned down. The Germans searched the island systematically. In many instances, Georgian prisoners were made to dig a large hole, were forced to take off their German army uniforms (which they had dishonored, according to the Germans), were shot, and were buried in the grave they had dug themselves. Torture was common. Finally, the fighting came to an end on May 20 when Canadian troops arrived and collected the weapons of the Germans, two weeks after the occupiers had capitulated in the remainder of Holland. During those two weeks, the Germans still behaved as if they were in charge. The number of casualties was large: more than 100 Dutchmen were killed (mostly due to artillery fire), 565 Georgians, and 800 Germans (who also had 500-plus wounded). There was major damage to farms and homes across the island.

We went by car to Den Helder, which was about 160 kilometers away and then across the Marsdiep to Tessel. When we got off the ferry, dad opened the roof window; and here and there, we could see the dunes with a slate-gray sky above them. I smelled or maybe imagined the salty sea air. Our vacation home turned out to be very nice and not far from the dunes, the beach, and the North Sea. The farm lady spoiled us with her cooking—in particular, her desserts. We made tours around the island and saw that there was still visible damage from the fighting. We ran around in the dunes and swam in the sea. I remember how cold it was. Flotsam, probably coming from ships sunk in the war, had accumulated at the edge of the water. I was in my I-want-to-be-a- biologist period and was happy to find different shells on the beach, and I identified plant species in the dunes. We even tried to catch dune rabbits with a catapult, and the bunnies just laughed at us. There was not much to do in De Koog, the village where we were staying, except for the pony cart. We all loved the pony cart, but we had to pay or give the owner a cigarette for a ride up and down Main Street. We had no money, so we had to find a way to get cigarettes. One of us got the idea to collect cigarette butts. We found the butts (the bus stop was a productive place), cut the butts open, and took the remaining tobacco out. We borrowed dad's roller box and rolled pretty decent-looking cigarettes. We made enough cigarettes that all of us got several pony rides.

Birds and Bees

With no longer in danger of air attacks, we spent a lot of our free time exploring the land outside of the dikes, which was more or less dry during the summer, when the river was at its lowest. It was very fertile (thanks to the periodic flooding), and a variety of plant species was growing there. Grass was abundant, and often the farmers would let their cows graze there.

One day, we were snorting around there, some friends and me. Pete was maybe two years older, and Wim was about the same age as me. Farther into the grass was a bull climbing on the back of a cow. Pete asked if I knew what they were doing, and I answered that they were playing some game. He started laughing and then explained in detail the story of the birds and the bees, making sure that we understood that humans played the same game to make a baby. Wim started screaming at him, saying that his parents would never do some crazy thing like that, but I knew instinctively that his story had to be true. I thought it was one of the funniest things I ever heard and laughed all the way home. Frankly, that thought had kind of stayed with me.

Pets

Once the war was over and we were back in our own house, we quickly accumulated quite a collection of pets. Most were rodents, guinea pigs, hamsters, rabbits, and mice. There were also tropical fishes, salamanders, and other critters. They came and went. But Mollie, a small black-and-white terrier-like dog, came and stayed for the duration. He was a tramp, showed up on our doorstep one day, and decided to move in; but he stayed a tramp. And during the day, he would be gone, and you could bump into him all over Gorinchem. When my mom went shopping, he liked to go with her; but she tried to avoid that because invariably, he would get into a fight with another dog, usually bigger than he was. One time, this happened inside a fancy store with many fragile items. It was a miracle that nothing was broken. Mollie was smart; and as soon as he saw my mom grabbing her bag or her coat, he would find some way to get out of the house by the front or basement door or by a window and hide and wait for mom at the corner of the street. When she passed by, he would follow her. At night, he would disappear, and it would take a while to figure out where he was. He would crawl under the blankets with us and lie flat between our legs, only visible if you pulled the blankets off.

To pay for feeding all those pets, we collected old newspapers, bottles, and so on and sold them to a man whose business was trading in recyclables. After paying us, he would send us inside his house to his wife who would get us some lemonade or tea and some cookies. There was a round table in the middle of the kitchen with a chandelier in the middle above it. They had a small monkey, which was free, and his favorite thing was to hang from the chandelier. He would piss, and of course, it would land on the table. The lady of the house would wipe it off the table with her hand onto the ground and say, "Oh, that is nothing, just clean water."

Eating Bird Eggs and Cat

The winter of 1945/46 was bitter cold. It snowed often, and the small Linge River was frozen solid. Even the much-wider Merwede River—some five hundred meters across—was frozen except for a ten-meter-wide channel in the middle, which was kept open by icebreakers to avoid the formation of ice dams with associated flooding. The cold and snow did not keep us at home and did not stop our explorations. One day, two of my younger brothers, Kees and Jan, were at a farm when the farmer had just shot a feral cat that had been after his chickens. My brothers asked if they could have the dead animal, which was kind of skinny, and they took it home. They skinned it and cleaned it and stuck it in one of our mom's frying pans. After it was done, all of us ate it; and other than being a bit gamy, it tasted pretty good. When the weather finally became warmer, we went up the Linge again in our canoes to look for duck and crow eggs. Duck eggs tasted fine, but they had to be cooked very well because they were frequently contaminated with Salmonella bacteria. The nests of the ducks were easily found at the edge of the water between the reeds.

We never took all the eggs from a nest, and the ducks would not abandon it. Getting crow eggs was another matter because it required climbing to the top of tall trees where they had their nests. We stopped collecting them as it was too much trouble to get them. Moreover, they tasted awful.

CHAPTER FOURTEEN

Gymnasium Camphusianum

AFTER FOUR MONTHS of freedom, it was time in September to get serious. The Gymnasium was a very academic classical high school, not very different from the first years of college in the USA. It was a small school. When I attended it, the total student body from year 1 through 6 was never greater than about, one hundred. My entering class of twenty-four students was the largest in years, possibly because of the war. Many kids had been unable to enter the Gymnasium during the last war year, creating a backlog. Ironically, I was younger than usual. Thanks to the private lessons I received when schools were closed, I had been kept up to date. I was not quite eleven and was two years younger than most of the students. Thus, I profited from the war, although in retrospect, it would have been better if I had been older and more mature to take advantage of the schooling. I took an admissions exam, and I passed it. So Mom dressed me in a sailor suit and sent me off to school.

The school ran from 8:30 a.m. to 4:30 p.m. with an hour for lunch, for which I went home. The school was located on a second floor above an elementary school. It had only six classrooms; and for some subjects—such as art, science, and gymnastics—we had to go to another school. The gymnastics took two hours per week, and the rest was academic. The school's excellent reputation was certainly not based on the facilities but on the high quality and dedication of the teachers, several of which had advanced degrees.

I will not describe all the teachers in detail. After all, the essence of this book was not just about the Gymnasium.

The rector was Dr. Endenburg, who also taught the classics. To me, it seemed that he ran a well-organized school although he did not teach any of my classes and I did not see much of him. Ms. Braakensiek taught French, and she was a unique woman with a very artistic personality. When I was in second grade, she wrote a long play (in French) about Sleeping Beauty and Mr. Bennis (the teacher of physical education) designed several ballets to go with the play. We practiced in school, and the play was to be presented at the annual school meeting. I can still remember one sentence of the play: *"Nous sommes les cuisiniers et nous avons preparé un bon diner pour le Roy et la Reine et leurs invites en honneur du bapteme."* I had been given the honor of waking up Sleeping Beauty by kissing her, a prospect I found terrifying. All went well except that my kiss ended up being an air-kiss, about a foot away from Beauty's face. Ms. Braakensiek also made a deal with me that every time I would take an exam or a test with a positive result, she would teach me a dirty word or a curse in French. I found out later that the words she taught me were pretty benign. But the strategy she used to get me to do my French work was pretty slick. She was always impeccably dressed but in a style that reminded me of the 1930s movie divas— small buttoned-up boots with high heels, skirts almost to the floor, a stylish blouse, and a jacket with a shawl on top. She was frequently smoking in class from a cigarette holder that was about a foot long. Rumor had it that she had a pet goat, which was kept in a cabinet in her living room. I had never seen the goat, so I couldn't vouch for the truthfulness of the story.

Another teacher who was very clear in my mind was Mr. de Graaf, who taught Latin and classical Greek. He tended to be somewhat impatient with me and not very happy when I, again, had not finished my homework. He would tell me to wait for him after school, and while we walked to his home, he would drill me on Latin verbs. Upon reaching his home, he would make me wait some minutes outside, and the ritual would start all over while we walked a short distance to the next destination of Mr. de Graaf.

Chemistry was the topic that I liked most partially because I was trying to set up my own lab at home and partially because the teacher, Mr. van Wagensveld, often came up with fascinating or even spectacular experiments, albeit not all were planned. More than once he did put his coat on fire because he lectured standing with his back against a workbench across the front of the class. The bench always had one or more lighted Bunsen burners on it, and Mr. van Wagensveld would lean back, putting the back of his coat into the flame. That led to him jumping up and down, trying to get his coat off to extinguish the flames. One of the most interesting experiments consisted of making beer in the classroom, topped off by an excursion to a beer factory in Breda by bus, some twenty-five kilometers away. We toured the factory and ended up in the high point of the trip—the tasting room. One day, the teacher demonstrated how a combination of an oxygen-producing compound and a fuel would burn. He mixed in a bit of iron powder as a catalyst. The mixture was placed in the middle of a sheet of paper, which in turn was placed on top of a tripod inside the fumes cabinet. He lighted a corner of the paper and closed the window of the fumes cabinet. The edge of the flame crept slowly closer to the mixture. It reached the powder on the paper, and a huge flame shot up toward the top of the cabinet. And suddenly, *boom!* There was an explosion. The shards of the glass cabinet window flew toward the students who, by this time, were on the floor under their benches. The windows in the outside wall also exploded, but outward. The director of the school came running to find out what on earth had happened. Luckily, no one was hurt.

After the fourth year, the class was split in two divisions—Alpha and Beta. Alpha students got more humanities and languages, while Beta meant more sciences. I picked Beta at the advice of my dad and ended up as the sole male in a class with five women, all two to three years older than me. I confess that I did not hesitate to scandalously abuse their maternal instincts, and I gladly accepted their help with homework all the way to simply copying their work. And thus, with their help and the push of my teachers, I made it to the sixth and final grade, never having to duplicate a year.

The final examinations were coming up. They were given by our own teachers and amplified by external examiners, usually university professors. After a week of exams, to my amazement and that of many others, I heard that I had passed.

To celebrate, we were invited to the homes of all the teachers, and I tasted my first *jenever* (Dutch gin) and got a bit drunk.

I had thought about what to do next, but my ideas came and usually were rapidly discarded. I thought about being a field biologist or joining the Dutch navy. The most attractive and logical choice was the family business— medicine. With a dad and three uncles as physicians, a mom and an aunt as nurses, and many cousins in various medical branches or studying medicine, I might as well join the crowd—a reasonable decision. It meant to go to the alma mater of most of them—the University of Amsterdam.

CHAPTER FIFTEEN

My Parents

Fig.15-1: My father's last photo shortly before his death

Fig.15-2: My mother as a young woman, just before she got married

MY DAD, Johan Thomas Zwaan, was born in 1905 in Djokjakarta in the Dutch

East Indies (now Indonesia), where his dad, my grandfather, was a mission minister for the Dutch Reformed Church. He was proud to be the very first "called" minister in Indonesia. Dad and his six brothers returned to Holland for their university education, and all seven ended up with doctoral degrees, quite a feat on a minister's salary. My dad started a family practice in Gorinchem, which initially was slow going, but it gradually grew to one of the largest practices in the city.

When Holland was occupied by the Nazis, my dad refused to sign up as a member of the *artsenkamer*, an organization meant to replace the Dutch Medical Society and set up to control the activities of the Dutch physicians. He also refused any collaboration with the anti-Semitic measures. In 1943, he was found guilty of anti-German ideas and attitudes and was sent for three months to the Nazi concentration camp in Amersfoort. I have no knowledge when he joined the resistance, and I believe it was quite early in the war. But he never talked about it. As a physician, he did not want anything to do with weapons, and his activities involved helping

Jews to escape from the Nazis by finding them hiding places to disappear safely until the end of the war. I was told a story by one of dad's acquaintances very much in line with my dad's thinking, although I can not vouch for its truth. A traitor of their Resistance Group had been caught and was locked up in a houseboat anchored in the middle of the Biesbos, a very large area of marshes, reeds, and water on the Southside of the Merwede river. The Group discussed, if they should execute the traitor and most members were in favor. My dad was strongly opposed against it and proposed that they keep the guy locked up on the boat and turn him over to the authorities after the liberation. He won.

Later he also helped pilots and other personnel shot down over Holland either to get away via the escape routes to Spain or after the Normandy landing by the Allied troops to liberated territory or to hide underground. This was not easy because few people dared to take the risk of being shot. Dad used any means available. A few years ago, a nephew pointed out a website to me from the Vancouver Holocaust Education Centre. It showed a photo of a doctor's note from my father, in which he stated that Mr. Albert Jacob van Haren could not be transported to German labor camps because of a heart condition that prevented him from doing heavy labor. That gave him and his family a few weeks to hide and "disappear." They survived the war and immigrated to Canada; and I assumed that this way, the note ended up in Vancouver, although the Centre, when asked, had no idea where the note came from.

My dad received a number of awards for his humane actions. One was from General Eisenhower on behalf of President Truman thanking him for the gallant work he did to assist Allied pilots and other personnel shot down over Holland to escape from the Nazis. He got similar recognition from Field Marshall Montgomery from the British side and from Yad Vashem in Jerusalem for his work with the Jews. A street was named after him in our hometown.

In many ways, he was a difficult man—very principled and taciturn—and his patients came first. For my mom, that must sometimes have been difficult. In 1954, he needed a cholecystectomy. Friends recommended that he go to Utrecht or Rotterdam, both of which had advanced medical centers, only some thirty kilometers from Gorinchem. He chose to go to the small local hospital because "what is good enough for [my] patients is good enough for [me]." He died during the surgery probably due to botched (ether) anesthesia. A photographer had taken his photo sometime earlier, and several hundred copies were sold to patients; the funds helped to pay for his gravestone. It was estimated that at least five thousand people lined the funeral route.

My mother, Johanna Zwaan-de Kok, was born was born in Den Helder in 1909. My parents lived not too far from each other. They were first cousins, and they knew each other for a long time.

Mom worked as a nurse in the navy hospital. My grandmother, Johanna de Kok, ran an old-fashioned drugstore; and I remember the dried chamomile and dandelions she sold and the cinnamon smell. *Opa* de Kok have a painting-contract business. After dad finished his studies, my parents got married, and they moved to Gorkum to start a family practice. Their first years there were quite tough economically; so they boarded a cousin, Dr. Adriaanse, who taught at the Gymnasium, to help with the expenses. My mom, very quickly, became pregnant; and dad, assisted by one of his brothers, did the delivery at home, as was the custom then. Unfortunately, the baby did not survive as the umbilical cord was wrapped around his neck. Otherwise, I would have been baby number two instead of being the oldest child. I was convinced that this event was a catastrophe for mom and that this influenced the rest of her life. Family members told me, that she was always laughing and doing things. For instance, she loved to play on the Zeedijk, jumping from one huge boulder to another, looking for the little sea snails near the sea, pick them out of their hells and eat them.

The practice had grown considerably, and dad got very busy. He was gone quite often, sleeping at different addresses to avoid being picked up by the Gestapo. Just imagine being a thirty-four-year-old mother with four boys from age five to eight and a fifth baby on the way and you see your husband being put on a train toward a concentration camp, not knowing when, or even, if he would return home.

The older I got, having children and grandchildren of my own, the more my admiration for mom had grown. She kept her cool under very tough conditions, and therefore, we kids did. Sure, there was panic when the air- raid alarms started up or when a V-1 came *put-put-putting* over. But once we were home, we were safe, and it became an adventure. I have asked all my brothers, and we agree that none of us did remember having had any lasting fear.

Us kids were always on mom's mind, and even at the end of her life, when she needed to be in assisted living, she would tell anybody close by that she had to go home to make dinner for her kids. She died in 1987.

I am grateful to both my parents for letting us grow up with an amazing degree of freedom that, in retrospect, was unbelievable and that allowed us to grow up as rather independent people.

Fig 15-3 Street named after my father

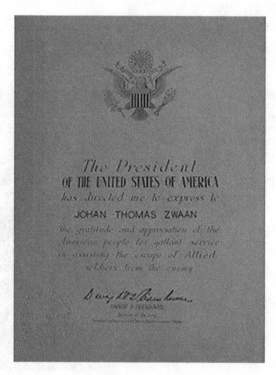

Fig 15–4: Letter from Gen. Eisenhower, received by dad

Johan Zwaan was born in Gorinchem, Holland, in 1934. He lived there during the occupation of Holland by the Nazis from age 5 to 10 years. Later he attended the local classical high school Gymnasium Camphusianum, which he completed at the age of 16. He attended medical school at the University of Amsterdam. His studies were interrupted, when he was drafted in the Royal Dutch Army in 1954. After his discharge from the Army he returned to Amsterdam in 1956. In 1960 he received the MD degree and three years later the PhD for research started in medical school. The day after the defense of his thesis he left for the United States for a one year postdoctoral fellowship in Pediatric Research at Johns Hopkins Medical School. After seven years at the University of Virginia he became a faculty member at Harvard Medical School. He missed contact with patients and Harvard gave him three years leave, and at age 40 he entered an Ophthalmology training program in Albany, NY. On completion he returned to Harvard for another 10 years, this time in the Ophthalmology Department. In 1988 he moved to the University of Texas in San Antonio as a Professor of Ophthalmology, Pediatrics and Cellular and Structural Biology. After 7 years he was invited to join the King Khaled Eye Specialist Hospital in Riyadh, Saudi Arabia. Three years later, in 1998, he returned to San Antonio and entered private practice. He retired in 2017. During his career he published numerous scientific and clinical papers, book chapters and a textbook, "Decision Making in Ophthalmology"(in 2014). After retirement he took up non-medical writing.

CPSIA information can be obtained
at www.ICGtesting.com
Printed in the USA
LVHW030759090721
692197LV00005B/573